BILL G

THE STORY OF MY LIFE

Revised June 2014

FOREWORD

This autobiographical book is in three parts. The first two, form a complete account of my father's life with the earliest part being up to 1952 when he was aged 32. This part might be better described as "The Story of My Preparation for Life". The last part is really an appendix or a travelogue of his travels to the far side of the world in the autumn of his years. I have included it as it shows his energy and enthusiasm for life and is as good a testimony as any to his indomitable spirit

My father Bill Grigg died in 1998 of prostate cancer aged 78. This book he wrote of his life was mainly completed by his own hand in the last few years of his life. There were also numerous tape recordings that he had made as he had become too ill to write and there were many additional notes and writings that he made of his travels to the Far East, Australia and New Zealand. The task I undertook of finishing it by writing up his travel notes and of his recordings has been a lengthy one. I admit it has taken longer than I originally wished.

Bill Grigg was a farmer who never travelled until his late sixties, he lived a full life and was a very well known and popular man. He was a Cornish farmer who struggled against setbacks and difficulties to make as full as life as possible for his family. He lived through a century of great changes and this book for the most part is a description of a country life now lost and his part within that community of yesteryear. The true legacy of this book; particularly in the writings of his early years; is his description of an age now gone, submerged by change and progress. I am sure that he would be pleased with his book if you are taken back to such a time and find pleasure from his recollections.

His kindness and generosity shone through to many that knew him. Those readers who knew my father will I hope obtain pleasure from this book. To those readers who did not know him I can do no better than offer my own thoughts of what sort of man he was. At his funeral I spoke a tribute of him which is noted at the end of this book. Rudyard Kipling's poem IF is also included; his favourite, which at times he would enjoy reciting in full to the amusement of his friends

I hope you enjoy reading of his life. It may give you some indication of who walked with us for a while and how fortunate some of us were in knowing this selfless man and how blessed I was in having such a man as my father.

Trevor Grigg – July 2003

PART ONE

PART TWO

PART THREE

PART ONE

EARLY MEMORIES

MY GRANDFATHER, William Ridgeman Grigg, after his marriage to Mary Baker went to live at Iresoke Farm, Boscastle, a windswept bleak farm of no more than fifty acres overlooking the Atlantic. My dad Richard Grigg was born there. After a few years they took over a farm at Kyrse, Treneglos some eight miles further inland. My dad and his brother John and two sisters Mary and Annie were all farming and living at Kyrse until my grandfather passed away at seventy years plus. My Aunt Mary was married late in life to a local man Edmund Turner. There were no children from the marriage. Aunt Annie was never married. Uncle John had two children, Mary and William both are at Kyrse today and farming.

During my dad's early years his father drove cattle from Kyrse to Bodmin for the annual St Lawrence Fair. The journey being 20 miles, they called at Stone Farm, St Mabyn, to rest the animals overnight, completing the journey the following day. It was through this venture that my parents met. My mother's family, the Wearys, farmed at Stone Farm. After some time this young farmer from North Cornwall came more frequently to Stone Farm to court my mother and eventually they were married at St Mabyn Church by the Reverend Allsopp who was a friend of the family. Many years later he became the vicar of my parish of Warbstow. After their marriage they moved to Trewen Farm, Pipers Pool, near Launceston where my brother Richard and I were born, Richard in 1916 and myself on 26 March 1920.

My mum's father, William Weary, I just remember from my holidays at Stone Farm, St Mabyn. He married a Miss Worden of Treveddoe Farm, Warleggan near Bodmin. There was a large tin mine in the valley below Treveddoe and my ancestors worked the mine up to approximately the 1940s and in the early days hauled tin ore to St Austell and Par Docks by horses for shipment abroad. On marriage my grandfather started with a smallholding at Helland near Bodmin. My Aunt Adelaide and my mum were born at Helland, the family moved from there to Stone Farm, St Mabyn, where my uncle Herbert was born (Herbert George Weary). Adelaide never married and died aged 58 years in 1938. My Uncle Herbert died in 1919 at 25 years of age. I believe he died because of his war wounds. He was in the Great War of 1914-18 in the Devon Yeomanry, serving abroad in Mesopotamia and India.

My mum spent some of her younger days looking after her granny at Minsey Down, Bolventor. At home she and her sister had to do the housework in the mornings and during the afternoons were expected to settle down to do embroidery, knitting, drawing, music etc; their mother was apparently well organised with a lot of drive and ambition for her children. I do not remember her she died around 1925.

I have seen photos of my mother when she was a young woman, of Band of Hope garden parties being held on the lawn at Stone. The ladies looked very elegant wearing long ankle-length dresses with large hats and tight bodices. Stone House was very spacious, with a walled rear garden, a front lawn with a walnut tree (now gone), a cork tree, yew tree and other shrubs, and made an ideal setting for these sorts of grand summer occasions. Shooting parties were also organised during the time that my uncle Herbert was a young man before the Great War.

My dad age 20 in 1909

*Uncle Herbert
(d 1919 age 25)*

My Mother

Edwardian Garden Party at Stone Farm (c1910)

MY EARLIEST recollections as a small child of the farmhouse at Trewen was it being set back on a bit of an incline from the village road and having to cross a very rocky uneven surface to reach the house. I remember that in a little thatched cottage just below on the other side of the road lived Mr and Mrs Sampson Couch. They had a parrot and this parrot fascinated me. I used to go down as a small boy, shake the gate, and Mrs Couch used to come out and let me in. 'I've come to see the parrot,' I would tell her. I'd go in and 'Hello' the parrot used to say to me, 'Hello'. It was quite fascinating. I was only one or two years old.

Me age 3

I also used to push my little wooden wheelbarrow around on the village road. I recall the local doctor, a Dr Budd giving me a good telling off once. By the church there was quite a sharp bend and he came round the bend in his car, of course it was unusual to see a car in those days, and I was there with my little wheelbarrow pushing it along. I recall this so vividly as only a few months ago I came across the broken remains of my old wheelbarrow lying in the disused loft of a barn. We both reached old age together but I think I was in the better condition.

We were only farming at Trewen for two or three years before moving to Fentrigan Farm in the parish of Warbstow. It was bought by my dad in 1921 for £3000. Fentrigan is two hundred acres of good fertile land rising to 800ft above sea level with views of the Atlantic and Lundy Island. On a clear day it is possible to see all three Westcountry moors Exmoor, Dartmoor and Bodmin. The farm has been in the Grigg family since the 1500s, previously as tenant farmers to the Duchy of Cornwall. Prior to Duchy ownership the manor farm was owned and farmed by monks and probably used as a resting place when travelling between monasteries. Henry VIII and the Reformation disposed of the monastic lands and transferred the properties held by the monks to the Duchy.

Before my dad took over the farm, his uncle Richard Grigg and his wife Fanny were tenant farmers there, they had no children. The farm was in a dilapidated state when my dad took it over. Richard Grigg was a cripple and was not keen on modern methods. It was the custom in those days that the tenant or occupier was expected to haul sand, stone and gravel by horse from the local beaches, for the purpose of building and modernising the farm buildings which were being financed by the Duchy. He declined to take on this responsibility. The Duchy tired of such a tenant and the farm buildings were so dilapidated that they sold the farm to my father. My dad made some improvements on a limited scale; money was very scarce, especially in the 1920s and 1930s. Life was very hard. No electricity, water only available from a well with a hand pump made of lead. Because of my great uncle's apathy it has taken three generations to modernise the farmhouse and buildings.

In the first year or two of farming at Fentrigan there was a fair amount of travelling between the two farms, a distance of some ten miles along roads and tracks. My mother was an accomplished horsewoman and we used to travel in a rallye trap with a fine well-groomed bay hackney. I remember sitting in this trap one night, mum and dad up front and my brother and I sat down below under the cover. Looking out from under the cover I remember seeing the moon above flying past the clouds, I thought to myself how strange that the moon was still there, it didn't seem to be moving and I did not understand.

Then another time I heard these bells and I asked my dad and mum, who were sitting up on front, about them as I was worried as to what the bells were. 'It's all right,' they replied, 'it's only the Colonel's Jersey cows.' They had little bells round their necks, and when they were grazing the bells used to ring.

These are my earliest memories of travelling on what was a short cut home in the early days of living at Fentrigan. Little did I know then, at the age of two that Fentrigan was to become my work, my home and my life. I was never to leave it and it was never to leave me.

Having settled in the new surroundings, I remember the vastness, the isolation, the long potholed lane and the overall dilapidated state of the farm buildings. In the front of the farmhouse was a small walled lawn, the wall four feet high with Delabole slate coping. A large monkey tree stood in the central area, with flower beds around the outside. A small iron gate gave entrance to the lawn area, with a pebble path to the entrance door. I recall two large upright granite pillars, probably the remains of a wagon house, with no roof, no doubt collapsed with age, situated in front of the lawn area. A small pond lay beyond.

To the right of the farmhouse, and at right angles, were stables with six stalls where the working horses were housed. The floor was of pebbles, with a loft 'tallet' over to accommodate the fodder. The loft floor, being aged, gave way to the weight and was quite dangerous. Going through the floorboards could land you in the company of a frightened horse. A small distance away the shippon housed twenty cows tied to wooden 'stiddles', very close together, a very narrow house with wooden mangers and a pebble floor. The loft above and the roof were in a state of collapse. When cleaning out the cowshed, dung was forked out through a hole in the wall. The roof of this shippon was unique, being of hand-sawn oak timbers, probably built a few hundred years ago of unseasoned timber, thereby giving the roof area irregularities and undulations. One wonders how it stood the test of time.

I clearly recall my great uncle Richard and his wife Fanny. He married very late in life and his wife, a wonderful generous woman, originated from Plymouth. We had not long taken over from him at Fentrigan and they had already retired and gone to live at Tredarrup a small neighbouring farm of a few acres. It was easy for a small boy like me to visit them at Tredarrup as it was only half a mile away along an infrequently used farm track. Fanny, a lovely kind lady in her sixties with long white hair, used to have a man called Morrish to help out on their small farm. I remember him as a pleasant friendly man.

I was quite a small boy, only three or four and I used to go out there sometimes and shake their front gate and Fanny would come out, open the gate and would always give me a penny and my brother the same. Her husband then in his seventies and crippled with old age was a tight old scrooge. I remember no pleasantries from him. He'd put his hand in his pocket for some money for us children and it wasn't often he'd pull out anything at all. I would often hear him bellow 'Fan! Fan! Somebody at door,' from either his bed or from sitting in his chair in front of the fireplace whilst we children would be shaking his gate or knocking on the door. His wife would always greet us with warmth.

Sometimes I would go in, both were old and getting on in years and were only farming in a small way with help from Morrish outdoors and a local maid called Mabel Watkins indoors. The filth inside was incredible, sheets, towels, blankets black with dirt and Mabel supposedly there helping. My mother used to help out as well, but rather infrequently, they all did it for a purpose, their thinking was 'What will the old cantankerous bugger leave us when he dies?' My mother got nothing and Mabel had the largest piece of the cake. She eventually got the house after Fanny died. Mabel was forever after referred to by my mother as 'that woman'.

I remember the death of my great uncle. I was only about ten years old and I was sent from his deathbed by my dad with urgency, told to go at great haste on a horse to my grandfather at Kyrse farm some five miles distant. I galloped full speed to deliver the message to my grandfather that his brother was dying. He eventually came to see his brother who died soon after. He had been bedridden for quite some time and I remember seeing him on his deathbed, a sight I would never forget, whiskers all over his face, hair everywhere, so unkempt and filthy in appearance. And of course there was the dirt, filthy sheets all smelling of urine and faeces.

On another occasion my father who used to keep some shire horse mares would need a mare taking to the stallion. If the mare was ready for a stallion I was asked, when about nine or ten years of age, to ride this mare to Mr Ward's farm near Camelford and was given general directions. I had no idea where Camelford was, I was so young, I put a bag on the horse's back, jumped on the back of the horse, and rode bareback to the farm, which was about seven to eight miles across Davidstow moors. Eventually I found the farm and Mrs Ward asked me in for a bit of lunch and something to drink. I gladly accepted her kind offer, got off the horse, went indoors, sat down, and had a meal with her two sons John and Bill. She gave me a piece of pasty, I have never forgotten it as I enjoyed it so much. But when she asked me if I wanted any more pasty, I very foolishly said 'No thank you Mrs Ward,' having been told to mind my manners when in strange company, but my God I wish she'd asked a second time because I would have taken her up on it, it was a beautiful pasty.

The mare being served, I made my way back home, still hungry, but having learnt a lesson from Oliver Twist in future 'ask for more'.

On another occasion a man called John Green, used to lead the stallion from Mr Ward's, and he used to come around to various farms and meeting places. Wainhouse Corner was one such place for farmers to bring their mares to be served by Mr Ward's stallion which was the only one of suitable breeding and quality in the district. My father used to go the few miles to Wainhouse Corner nothing more than a crossroads and a few houses to get his mares served. It was certainly a lot quicker and more convenient than the alternative long trek across Davidstow moor to Mr Ward's farm.

Wainhouse Corner was also a suitable venue for holding a livestock market. I remember one occasion when it was pouring with rain, terrible weather, with horse and cart driving some cattle the four miles from the farm to the makeshift market. When you arrived there were no pens or anything, you just had to try your best to hold the livestock whether it was sheep, cattle or pigs up against the hedge in a corner of the field. Even when the auctioneer came along and sold them, generally speaking in those days you had to take them home again and keep them for a fortnight before the fatstock buyer would organise the train. Then you would have to drive them again the few miles to Otterham Station to be loaded on a truck for their destination.

In my early years my dad introduced some Aberdeen Angus cattle to the farm, I remember going to Killivose Farm, near Truro, to a Mr and Mrs Richards who had a number of Aberdeen Angus, some pedigree. We arrived I remember by car and were first invited to join them for lunch. I was about ten years of age I suppose, and what I remember most was meeting Mrs Richards, she was an artist, a beautiful artist and I had never met an artist before. In their large drawing room she had painted a frieze about two feet high at the top of the walls. It went all around the room, it was a hunting scene, with horses and hounds and the fox and as you went around the room so you went through woods and various landscapes. I was really impressed, she was great and she had one large special room that she took me into and gave me a little guided tour. It was full of various portrait paintings of people that she had painted. The room overflowed with her work, many were hung but several were placed on the floor.

After all these preliminaries eventually we were shown some very beautiful beasts, cleaned and groomed for the occasion. My father made his choice of two heifers. The Angus have such beautiful faces, round of course, black, full eyes, and a docile nature, being small but bred especially for quality beef. After this purchase, we then followed on to Lord Falmouth's estate near Tresilian, meeting the farm manager, a Mr Shrimpton (whose daughter incidentally attended the same school as my sister, St Joseph's, Launceston), who took us around the buildings. These impressed me, being so large, well-maintained and housing these Aberdeen Angus cattle in such good clean condition. I told myself that things would not be so pleasant for them when removed to their new environment. However my father eventually, after a few haggles, bought a few more pedigree heifers. The next move was to get a bull of the same breed. My father bought this bull from the Duchy Farm used by Dartmoor prison at Belliver, near Princetown. The bull, a pedigree, was named Bellions Lad and I did not accompany my father at this time. However I recall the story of this bull being trucked to Launceston Station and breaking loose at the train station, getting onto the streets and causing mayhem. He was eventually rounded up and caught, no damage being done to people or property or my father's prize bull. Perhaps the bull had learnt something of escape from his former keepers.

SCHOOLDAYS & SMALL ADVENTURES

THE SCHOOL at Warbstow was my one and only school until I left at age fourteen; it was expected in those days that children left at the earliest opportunity to work on the farm. There was farm work to be done each morning and then off to school by walking two miles across very exposed fields in all types of weather. Tasks prior to school usually were milking cows by hand, separation of the milk to cream and, if time permitted, churning the cream to butter. There was a rushed breakfast of porridge, home-cured fat bacon and eggs, then off carrying a leather satchel with a pasty for school lunch, arriving late, never before 9.30. Then we were lined up in front of the class and schoolmaster would cane my brother and I across the hands for being late. Such are my memories of school.

I remember my first day at school, my brother being three and a half years older. There were two entrances to the schoolhouse. He went in his door and told me to enter the other door for the very junior children. I was nervous and shy and stood outside for a very long time until a boy reported me. The elderly schoolmaster came outside, picked me up and carried me through the classroom. I had never seen so many children in my life. He made such a fuss of me; I quite enjoyed the attention. Life at school was very different and difficult. We were given slates with slate pencils to write with in the earlier days.

We wore leather hobnail boots which, being made to measure, were quite supportive and sometimes we wore leggings. I remember being measured by the local cobbler Archie Stephens who lived in the highest house in Cornwall on Davidstow moor. This was for new boots and leggings for me to show off at school. The boots were hobnailed with scoots at the toe and heel. The new leggings were very tight fitting and going across the fields towards the school my calf began to swell because of the running and walking. The pain was so severe that I had to rest and lie on the ground until my calf relaxed and the pain subsided. No school that day. I slowly returned home to my parents.

One episode that stands out in my memories concerns a woman relief teacher with large breasts. I muttered in class as schoolboys do 'Every time she walks she wobbles' (whether she heard me I'm not sure). The class had been asked to do spellings. If correct one could call out a boy or girl's name to do the next spelling. I called out a boy called Fry and said 'Frying pan'. She took me aside and put me into a corner. She cleared the room of children then stood me on the form and gave me such a beating that I thought that she would never stop. The wall was at my back and I couldn't fall anywhere because she had me at all angles. The children were watching through the glass porch door. Eventually she became exhausted, went very quiet and walked away (being young I did not understand human nature then). The children were very sympathetic towards me. 'Why don't you go home?' I was afraid to do that just in case I should get another beating.

At school my nickname was 'Tuffy', probably because I was caned so often for being late for school without shedding any tears. I had a bicycle frame put on any two wheels if no cycle wheels were available. I would use pram wheels and a gin peg put in for the axle, there wouldn't be any tyres on the wheels, no chain for pedalling and a bag tied on for the seat. I would ride this boneshaker down the hill toward the school. On one occasion I was sailing along and all of a sudden the front pram wheel collapsed and the forks hit the ground. I somersaulted over the handlebars and landed unhurt. A number of children saw this and it caused a big laugh, but my problem was how to get another wheel, as they were in short supply. I had to hide the so-called bicycle from my dad, usually in a furzebush on the Burrow.

Warbstow Burrow was a man-made ancient iron age type of fort with dug-out ditches and very steep banks in the form of two to three rings, each of varying height. The banks were overgrown with furze bushes. During a break from school a few supporters would cheer me on when I took my famous boneshaker and myself through these furzebushes, having to do some weaving, if not one came to a sudden catastrophe amongst the prickles, giving an exciting time for all.

At the top ring of the Burrow is, as legend has it, a giant's grave, a large mound. Supposedly he was killed by another giant from Launceston Castle. However, returning from school with two or three other homeward bound kids, we decided to try whether we could hear the chains rattling by running around the grave for a number of times and then putting our ears to the ground and listening. However at that moment what we did hear was the galloping of a horse, making towards us kids with the farmer shouting and throwing his whip around. We immediately dispersed but unfortunately I, being the smallest boy, could not get away so easily. The farmer, Mr Dick Uglow, who caught me with his whip, went on his way to get the others. They dispersed in their own different ways. Some hid in the furzebushes. He was not a popular man.

Roy Cowling was a boy of my age, then about nine to ten years, who was a blacksmith's son from Canworthy Water. His father Alfie Cowling once poached salmon and, when being apprehended by the police, denied any knowledge of salmon in his possession. After a thorough search of his premises they left, not knowing that the salmon was in bed with his supposedly sick wife.

Me age 11

Roy and I, during a school lunch break, decided to take a couple of bicycles from the local quarry and have a ride around. He could ride a bicycle but I could only rest my foot on one pedal and hope for the best. Going down the hill he was in front and waiting for me when I caught up speed and could not stop and ran into the rear of his bike. This of course altered our well laid plan. His back wheel was buckled, my front wheel was also twisted and the pedal was bent. We took the bicycles, half carrying them, back to the quarry and returned to our classroom, apprehensive as to the outcome of this adventure. There came a knock on the door and an enquiry through the headmaster as to what culprits had made these bicycles partly wrecked and unusable. At first reluctant to admit our misdeeds, we eventually admitted our guilt and the outcome was that I had to pay £1 10shillings (150p) towards the costs of the damage otherwise the police would be called in. This was a lot of money in those days. Roy likewise had the same costs and a similar caution about the police. Talk of the police put the frighteners on me because this money had to be brought to school in full the following day. I was really worried; I dared not let my parents know. I returned from school and remember that I didn't want any supper that evening and the following day my mum thought I was sickening for something. To get the money was a big problem. I knew where our money boxes were kept (that is my brothers' and sisters') so I decided that I would try to creep around at a convenient time and see how much I could steal from that source. I was so scared of doing this but succeeded in getting together approximately £1 and took this to school the following day. The man came to school and I handed him the £1 and he reminded me that a further ten shillings was due the following day otherwise the police would be coming for me. I did get this ten shillings eventually and handed it over to my great relief. As the time and weeks went by I recovered from this experience until my mum called me in one day to the lower kitchen and, with a stick in her hand, asked me to tell the truth about the bicycle escapade. I told her, she asked how much it cost me and how I came to get the money. At first I said ' It cost me two shillings, mummy.' She said to me, 'I want the truth,' and I then told her that it cost me £1 10shillings and that was the truth. She asked me where I got the money from, warning me she would tell my dad if I did not tell her, all of which would have meant more inquiries and perhaps a good hammering into the bargain. I told her that I had taken it from the money boxes and that was the end of the matter. This experience taught me a lesson for the future that it is better to come clean and to tell the truth.

I well remember the local village blacksmith and rabbit trapper; he was called Traige, a tall lanky fellow with a queer sense of humour. His wife, Lilian or 'Lil' was a large plump woman who when talking would roll up her sleeves and at the same time make a gesture and a hearty laugh. I was rather cheeky one day to her, she chased me, but I easily outran her and got away. I had to take our pony 'Twinkle' at times to school in the mornings to get it shod at the blacksmiths. It had to be kept there for the day until out of school, I would collect the pony and make for home. On a few occasions Ed Dawe, living in our direction, would beg a lift to save walking over two miles to his home at Trelash. This pony of ours was very fast and the 'catch ups' made no difference to his speed. (Catch-ups meant the rear right leg would, on walking, lift up much higher than normal). Ed Dawe, being a fearless lad, would get up behind me and hold tight like grim death, the pony being keen and rearing and wanting to go. The two of us, settled on its back, releasing the reins and making for home at a full gallop, with no fear, arrived at a pre-arranged parting place. Drawing up on all fours he would dismount and I would continue homeward.

Prior to this I had experienced several falls from 'Twinkle' and heavy horses which made me experienced to a degree. Once when I was riding one of our carthorses with only a halter drooping across the neck, strolling in the farm lane, he suddenly leapt forward, throwing me back over. I hit my head on a large stone. The cause of this sudden plunge was the dog had that leapt out from the hedge. Cut and bleeding and slightly stunned I staggered to my feet and attempted to get to the farmhouse. The horse was at the stable door without a rider, and my dad already looking for me. I was taken indoors, sat on the settle with mother washing the blood from my face. I was stunned, becoming rather excited and starting to give details of what I was going to do to that horse. I was quietly put to bed and after a short spell recovered.

❖ ❖ ❖

My Aunt Mary

I HAD two aunts Mary and Annie and a grandfather who lived and farmed at Kyrse a few miles from home.

This was my father's side of the family. On my mother's side I had Aunt Adelaide a maiden aunt and my grandfather who both lived and farmed at Stone Farm near St Maybn. I remember as a boy of about ten or eleven at least I can't have been still in a total state of childhood innocence a prank played by the builders on my Aunt Annie who had never married. I was staying with my two aunts and grandfather at Kyrse. The builders were there, working on a project, when one of the lads, having a condom to spare, on passing the trap with the shafts in a raised position, rolled the condom over the point of the shaft and then went indoors for their lunch break. The carriage house adjoined the farmhouse and to enter the farmhouse one had to pass the parked traps. The two builders were sitting on the form inside the table and taking their food with whatever beverages were going when my aunt Anne came into the kitchen. 'Look, Mary, see what I have found stuck over the shafts,' holding up this French letter for all to see. 'What a good idea, this will protect my finger which was damaged yesterday.' She then proceeded to roll the condom over her finger. The two men, trying to keep a straight face, made a hurried retreat.

As a small boy, I did enjoy the visits to my aunts and grandfather. Every Christmas at Kyrse my aunts gave a party, my grandad's birthday being 1st January. We were given sweets and other luxuries that were normally in short supply at our house. They had a water wheel that was used for milling the corn for the cattle food. The large stone mill would make a distinct noise and it was being used all hours of night and day so long as the water supply held. The grinding process was laborious and terribly slow.

My grandmother Mary Grigg died 1926

I just remember my maternal grandfather from my holidays at Stone Farm. Every year as a holiday treat I would stay with grandfather and auntie, sometimes with my elder brother but frequently on my own. I believe I was my Aunt Adelaide's favourite, she had no children of her own and I was always made very welcome. I was then aged between three and four years and to me my dear old grandpa was quite old, possibly in his seventies. A large-built man, I remember, with a flowing beard and a husky voice, usually wearing a bowler hat and wearing breeches and leggings. Taking me by the hand he would walk me to the fields and, in my small way, I would attempt to help him, perhaps to keep the gate open while he moved the cattle to new pastures. He always took his walking stick, and his pipe was not often missing, but he was always very likeable and, to me at any rate, friendly.

The farm had lots of attractions to me, there were apple orchards, pear trees growing alongside the high enclosed garden wall, also a favourite Victoria plum tree situated in the corner of the garden. I would shake the tree and pick up these beautiful juicy plums and devour them. Taking walks was a favourite, especially along the winding narrow lanes; during the springtime there was an abundance of primroses and daffodils growing along the hedgerows and in my innocence this gave me a feeling of lasting beauty and a world full of wondrous things. Looking back one now appreciates the way nature inspires the simple quiet country life, and the flowers I gathered and proudly presented to my aunt, who appreciated the gesture, putting them on display and giving me a great sense of satisfaction.

Times have changed. Calling recently at the same area of which, as a boy, I had so many beautiful memories, it has now disappeared because of modern technology. The beautiful hedgerows have been bulldozed, removing the wild flowers. The peace and tranquility, which, as a boy, gave me such happiness and inspiration, has now gone and gone forever. The fields are now much larger, hedges removed, concrete and new buildings have taken over. The beautiful large elms are all gone because of Dutch elm disease. The orchards are no longer there, but in their place is a very large building to accommodate modern machinery and a milking parlour. The plum tree has gone, and those lovely pear trees no longer exist. How I enjoyed that lovely fruit, also the homemade apple jam, plum jam, all laden on scones with my aunt's home-made clotted cream. The cream had a very special flavour; the technique being to place a large pan filled with milk and slowly simmer it over a heated stove. After a time it was allowed to cool and then the top layer of cream skimmed off, it was thick, clotted and very tasty.

On the lawn there stood a walnut tree, since blown down by a gale. We gathered walnuts, stored them and cured them in the haystack before the Christmas feasts. In those days taking a place of honour in the lawn was a cork tree, and in the centre a poisonous yew tree. The cork tree still stands but gone are the dahlias that bordered the entrance drive, now down to grass and integrated within the lawn. Shrubs have been replaced; the old garden and lawn that once had such a fascination for me, where we would hide and play, spending many happy hours, has gone.

As a young boy I really looked forward to getting away from home and having a little holiday with my doting aunt. When a little older, I suppose seven or eight I would go by train the fifteen miles to St Kew station, and then walk the three miles to my grandparents farm. It was a large traditional farmhouse with slated floors and a large number of rooms. There were two kitchens; the big first kitchen had two coppers for washing with an aperture below for the fire, also a very large open hearth with a clome oven. I used to sit there by the open fire during my visit with my grandad and listen to the crickets chirping. This high room had a massive beam going through the centre and an approximately 18 feet long kitchen table. There was a large lounge with massive dressers and sideboard, a further long table like a banqueting table with forms, a slated floor, a black stove fuelled by wood or coal, and a gun rack above the hearth. The ceiling had a number of hooks where the hams used to be hung. There was an indoor lead pump and a larder.

During the Christmas period my aunt would arrange for a large amount of wood to be collected and then she and I would use the crosscut saw and the sawhorse to cut it into logs. New Year's Eve was a special treat, after working for hours, at midnight we would go outside and hear the church bells from three churches ringing out the old year and ringing in the new.

My grandfather's brother Edward Weary lived at Carwen, Blisland with his wife and only daughter Jenny, (who later married Harry Dingle, all now laid to rest in Blisland churchyard). Whilst on holiday I would sometimes walk the four or five miles to visit them at Carwen. I remember one occasion attending, with them, the church service on the Sunday prior to St Pratt's fair, an annual horse and sheep fair on Blisland Green that I recall being held on a Monday. My aunt had given me, prior to my stay at Carwen, one penny piece and a half-crown for spending money at the fair. At church when the collection was being taken I mistakenly put the half crown in the collecting box instead of my penny. This made me quite upset, and when leaving the church I wanted to go back and collect my half-crown and give them the penny. However all was resolved and the half-crown was reimbursed without any further embarrassment.

When I was about nine to ten years of age I was put on a train from the local station at Otterham to St Kew Highway Station. I was going to stay at my grandad's and auntie's farm at St Mabyn, approximately three miles from the stations. This was done on quite a few occasions, it was a long walk but I looked forward to being with my grandad. The train pulled up; I got out and went to the station porter with my ticket. He took me into a small room and started to play with my privates after dropping my trousers. Of course, being so young, I started to cry and after a time he stopped. Having got away, quite frightened, I went on with my journey, the three-mile walk to the farm. I do not remember saying anything to anyone. The next time I went on that same journey I became really frightened on getting near the station. I remember I planned to jump off the train before it stopped. I did not jump but as soon as the train stopped I flew out and across the station platform, so fast I don't suppose anyone saw me.

When staying at St Mabyn with my auntie and grandparents it was my job to visit the St Mabyn vicarage to pay the vicar the parish tithe money, the Queen Anne's Bounty, to a Rev Longmore. This was a tax, now obsolete, from the farms that helped to keep the priests.

ONCE my mum took me by horse and trap to St Luke's Fair garden party at Dozmary Pool on Bodmin Moor. I was a tiny boy and somehow I lost my mum, and there were all these ladies walking around with their long dark dresses down to their ankles and their big hats. And there was me, this little lost boy sitting at the water's edge watching the ripples and looking for mum. I remember tugging at a long dark dress thinking that was my mum but she looked at me, and no, it wasn't my mum. So on to the next one, to a small boy all the ladies were so similarly dressed. It was with great relief that, still at the water's edge, I clearly recall my mother picking me up into her arms.

I remember going with my mum to Minsey Down near Bolventor and meeting with a family whose name I forget. I was shown a well of about 40-50 feet deep and in the kitchen an open fireplace burning turf which was never allowed to go out. The turf was

Mum Baby Richard and Grandmother

cut on Bodmin Moor and stacked in a rick, dried and ready for use. I recall how tragic it was that this family had lost several young children through, I believe, consumption.

My mum and dad would organise annual summer church outings. This was usually a coach trip in what was known as a charabanc. On one particular trip to Newquay in a coach with wooden seats provided by Crowles Coaches of St Gennys I had been given sixpence to spend for the day. I was young and tempted by another passenger to try my luck at the one-armed bandit by the entrance to the beaches. He said: 'Put in one penny and you may get some extra money back'. However I learnt my lesson and I have never forgotten it. All my pennies were lost and there was no more spending money for the day. The ice cream and sweets looked so good but I was not to taste them.

Sunday was a day of rest with regular attendance at church for the whole family in our Sunday best, dad being a churchwarden always attended and I remember one Sunday having to collect Mr and Mrs Holden an elderly couple who were invited to Sunday lunch. I wasn't very old, only nine or ten, and had the responsibility of harnessing up this horse to the trap and taking it the few miles to collect them. They were ready, jumped in the trap and I drove them back to the farm, and indeed back again to their home later that day. That was a big experience for me, all part of growing up, and my God, you had to grow up fast in those days.

It wasn't often that I went to Launceston, fourteen miles away, but when I did go, as a small boy, I used to get some excited. I remember seeing these toys in the shop, boy oh boy didn't I want to get to those toys, didn't I want to grab hold of them. Anyway I went there and we bought some toys, took them home, and if we didn't play with them properly they would be taken away from us and we wouldn't see them again for a long time. Toys were handed down from one child to the other and the same with children's books. Christmas presents were handed down from child to child, usually after three years. We would all get a little something for Christmas, usually a toy like a little metal Dinky car or something and a few sweets. Those were our Christmas presents for us as kids.

One day when I was about five years old mother took me to Launceston and she put me in the cinema so that she could do her Christmas shopping. I had never been to a cinema before and on comes Mickey Mouse! Oh my God! What a scream, I started to jump up and down, get excited, people around me were getting really excited too for I believe this small boy gave more entertainment to the audience than the film. I hadn't seen anything like this in my life before. And then there was a silent film with a car being driven by a father and the daughter was sitting beside the father, and chained to her wrist was her boyfriend who was running alongside the car. As the car drove on, on the side of the pavements were boxes of oranges and apples, and of course the poor old boyfriend, he couldn't do anything but run, he had to jump over them, some of them he cleared and some he didn't, the oranges and apples all went rolling down the street. And of course he was still running alongside the car. Really, we were all thrilled to bits with me being the most excited. When my mother came to pick me up they didn't want the boy to leave, so people said, 'Let him stay, we love him, don't take him away'. I was kicking and yelling and saying 'I don't want to go', and they said 'No, don't take him away'. After that if ever my mother went to Launceston with me she kept me well away from the street with the cinema.

I remember my parents driving the trap over Davidstow moor coming home from Stone one evening, when a puff of wind came and blew my hat off. Of course, dad had to get off the trap in the darkness, go in over the hedge and try to find my cap, which he never did, and I remember I prized this hat because it had a special badge in front. I also remember wearing corduroy breeches with detachable swansdown linings that you could attach inside with buttons in times of cold weather.

At carnival time I got separated from my mum and it seemed like a lot of fun to me as a four- year-old to join in the procession. So there I was walking alongside Charlie Chaplin and really enjoying myself. She found me eventually, I can't remember if she was amused with me for clowning around.

Going with my mum to Bodmin from St Mabyn by horse and trap, we called at a cousin of mother's who kept a shop under the town clock at the lower end of Fore Street, Mr & Mrs Dumble. I was about three to four years old and, being rather bored, was left outside to watch the horses and carriages and a large number of people, ladies dressed in long dresses and large hats with their shopping baskets. The men wore bowler hats. Becoming excited with all the people and activities which I had not seen before, I decided to walk off. I remember wandering under an archway and going up the main hill which was Fore Street. On seeing this small boy on his own the women came from both sides of the street from their shop doorways, each asking who I was. 'Farmer Bill' was my reply and this caused quite a lot of laughter, bringing out still more shopkeepers and others inquiring as to who was this little boy in hobnail boots and corduroy breeches. Still the reply they received was 'Farmer Bill'. When I was halfway up the hill and still walking, a shout came from the bottom of the hill, 'Hi there, catch that boy!' I started to run away but was easily caught by one of my admirers and eventually handed to my rescuer, Mr Dumble.

Some years later as a schoolboy on holiday at St Maybn I would call upon some of these retired shopkeepers in the village of Helland as I was walking or cycling to Bodmin. Introducing myself as 'Farmer Bill' was always a sure way for them to recollect who I was. Sometimes when going by train to Launceston the coach and horses from the White Hart Hotel in the town square used to ferry passengers from the station and drop them off at the town centre as there was quite a steep hill to climb up beside the Norman castle which dominates the town. George was the horseman at the time, and he could charm warts. My father used to suffer terribly from warts on the back of his hands. His hands were literally covered with seeded warts, and mother used to burn them back with a red-hot poker. Anyway he tried this charmer George and George said 'When I charm them you just walk away, don't say anything, don't thank me, say nothing' Father had his warts charmed and he walked away, didn't say thank you or anything. After some weeks they all came off, the seeds came off, the warts went completely, no more problems.

As a teenager I had a large number of warts on various parts of my body. A lady at Camelford (Mrs Knight) told me to collect the same number of leaves from a blackcurrant bush. This being done, I took them to her. Saying something and at the same time threading them through with a needle and cotton she handed the threaded leaves to me. 'Take them home and bury them" she said, which I did. As the leaves rotted, so my warts disappeared.

Speaking of charms, our local postman, George Petherick of Canworthy Water would charm the ringworms on our calves without even seeing them. Another local lady could stop bleeding by charms. It was said that a charm would never work if it was passed on to the same sex (male to male, female to female).

I had a holiday, my first real break at twelve years of age, to Torquay. My aunt Adelaide, recovering from an illness, took me by train to a cousin's house where we stayed for a week or more. Excited at the journey by steam train from Bodmin Station to Torquay, I stood most of the way, looking out of the window, in the meantime becoming very black with the smoke from the engine covering my skin and new clothes.

Father was a quiet man, reserved, conservative, of few words and very patient. I used to get terribly frustrated with him as a teenager and young man. Mother also used to get a little heated with him at times. He seemed set in the old ways of doing things and brother and I wanted to progress, to adapt to new technology. He was capable of a dry sense of humour but he was slow to change his ways. He dressed in corduroy trousers, hobnail boots, and leggings, always the same, that was his style. He had a Sunday special pair of leggings and boots he used to wear to church. Mum used to wear long black dark clothes usually with an apron over when working. I remember the big hats she used to wear with pins going through her hat.

A few examples of my father's character are best described by some events that I recall being told to me. A farmer's car stalled going through a local stream. Father came on the scene with his horse and cart, not attempting to get off but just sat there enjoying his pipe of tobacco. After some considerable time the car driver, who was not making any progress towards getting out of the way, offered his apologies. All the response he apparently got from my father was: 'Time is going on, young man.' Another example of the calm quality of his nature was between him and Edgar Dawe, our farm worker. They were in the farmyard loading a wagon and Dawe was holding the horse. Father, typically without temper or urgency in his quiet voice, said: 'Dawe, move the horse forward, the wheel is on my foot.' He was a man of few words but when he spoke you knew that his words were thoughtful and full of meaning. I never saw him in a violent temper, never heard him swear, he was a calm and cool character with words of advice that I should have listened to a lot more than I did. Being young I had all the answers.

There was an occasion when I got lost on the farm as a very small boy and mum and dad went looking for me. After some time they found me asleep in a haystack with a pasty in my hand. I was only two or three years old. It was an adventurous sort of streak that I had always wanted to be doing something, wanted to be on the move somewhere.

HARVEST HOME

THE FIELDS of Fentrigan were all four, five or six acre fields enclosed with stone hedges and banks. These banks were loaded with rabbits. The land was mainly down to permanent pasture. The soil was free draining on the higher fields that were rather exposed rising to 800 feet above sea level. There were no granite outcrops but the base rock is an uncommon freestone, a type of shale or sandstone that can be cut with a handsaw. Just outside the farmhouse are the remains of an old quarry, and stone from here was used to build Treneglos church as well as being used to construct the farm buildings and the farmhouse.

When I was ploughing with horses I always took a shovel or pick with me and if I saw a stone I'd mark the spot with a stick and later I would go back and dig this stone out. If the plough being pulled by a team of two ever caught a large buried stone the plough would cartwheel right over or it would go to one side, catch you in the ribs and knock you over. The fields by modern standards were very small. To plough a five-acre field would take five days. Very few cereals were grown, just enough oats for our own use. It was mainly down to permanent grass and we had a rotation system but my father was a bit of a stickler for that. Two cereals, one root, seeded out and back to pasture again.

The material for thatching the ricks was whatever was to hand. In our district it was rushes. We would go up to Davidstow moor with our scythes, cut the rushes in all weathers, water running out the bottom of our boots, bind them up, put them on a horse and wagon and take them home and thatch with them. Reed or wheat straw was better than rushes but these were not available in our district, we couldn't grow wheat so we had to use rushes, which often let the rain in.

Summertime in the harvest fields was a special time for all the family. During late summer the binder, which was hauled by three heavy horses, entered a field to harvest the oats. It was customary to cut the corn by scythe around the outside of the field, so that the horses did not trample the corn to the ground. This corn had to be gathered and bound by hand. Cutting by the binder was an experience that I enjoyed, the smell of the golden corn waving in the breeze, being cut by binder with the power of three horses drawn alongside. Usually the youngest horse was in the middle, not being so experienced. The corn once cut, the beaters would lay the straw on to the canvasses which rolled the straw towards the rear of the binder to the tying mechanism where the sheaf was tied, with string being fed from the string box and the sheath kicked out on to the ground by an automatic trip. Our job as young boys was usually to gather the sheaves from seven rows and put them into one row with the ear end of the sheaf placed outward, ready for stooking into sixes and eights. The sheaves were left in the field for ten days to ripen before taking them to be put in a large rick, which was later thatched and eventually thrashed by machine (in earlier days barn thrashed with a metal knuckled hand beater). The thatching was done with rushes and long roping was preferred, especially with ricks being exposed to high winds. A large number of rats would get into the stooks and during the thrashing time, especially when the stack was nearly finished, a large gathering of men with sticks and dogs would assemble to kill off most of them. However a few would escape.

Rabbits were plentiful in the fields and, being scared of the noise of the binder, they would not attempt to escape from their cover until the area of cover was so small that there was no other way but to make a run for it. With many sheaves lying on the ground rabbits would run into them, and, confused, could sometimes be caught by people or dogs. Harvest was hard work but as young boys we used to get some pleasure and pocket money by catching rabbits. We would be there with our dogs ready to catch them and it was quite exciting. We used to catch these rabbits, kill them and sell them.

About teatime my mother would bring out the harvest hamper laden with rich homemade beef and onion pasties, perhaps an egg pastry tart coated with a sprinkling of nutmeg to give it flavour. There were also homemade buns and cake, homemade jam and cream by the spoonful. Everyone had their stories to tell and jokes were not in short supply. During this time the horses would have their rest.

During the war years one had to put small wire mesh netting around the ricks so that the rats could not enter. I've picked stones by hand from the arable fields and the smaller stones were used to keep the farm drive in good repair. Larger stones were used for hedge repairs. My grandfather remembered as a boy that oxen were used during the mid-1800s. We still have the oxen yoke on the farm. Our Massey Harris binder was imported from Canada (1888-1893) with an undercarriage. Back then some of the farm labourers went on strike because the binder was taking away their livelihood.

We had this old Massey Harris binder, several years ago I went to a man in Launceston to enquire about a spare part, he told us that this binder was quite rare and was introduced from Canada, from the serial number he could tell it was one of the first binders introduced in Cornwall, between 1888 and 1894, and all it needed was one big ball bearing in one of the wheels. I grew a lot of oats one year, I think it may have been 1965 and for whatever reason I wanted to use the binder rather than the normal combine harvester. We got the spare part, got the binder working and we cut the sheaves, stooked them up and brought them into the barn and made a rick

I remember the milking by hand of cows. Milking time with a bucket and stool, pushing your head into the lower flank of the cow and being sat between the cows (there being no stalls) was not a pleasant experience. One never knew what would happen when a cow kicked out, bucket, stool and the unfortunate milkman would be sent flying. In the pandemonium a sort of 'domino effect' would apply.

I well remember cleaning out the cowshed by fork through a hole in the wall, the dung would accumulate in a yard outside before being loaded up again by hand onto a cart and then spread again by hand onto the fields. Adjoining the cow shed was a chaff house, an engine house with a Blackstone engine (installed in 1888) which powered a mill for grinding corn, a chaff cutter and a barn thrasher with various unguarded pulleys and belts. When all these machines were working the noise and the pulleys and belts were literally all open to view. I now realize how very dangerous it was working in those conditions, especially by night with just a hurricane lantern to show the way.

To bring the uninitiated up to why this machinery was necessary, it was essential to get the sheaves (corn) to the barn from an outside rick and store for feeding the animals during the long winter months. Again I recall taking hay from a hayrick, cut in blocks with a hay knife with a long blade and wooden handle, a length of rope, made double, laid on the floor and wrapping the hay around with the rope, eventually getting the hay on one's back and proceeding to get it to the animals, sometimes at a distance.

During the summer the hay was brought into the mowhay with wagons hauled by heavy horses. To get the hay the correct quality at first the mower was used, turned by hand with a gang of either men, women or sometimes children who incidentally used to enjoy the work, especially in the early days. A tedder was used later as a substitute for forks. A horse rake took over from woodenhead rakes and sometimes when the weather was uncertain we were obliged to make it into pokes where it would dry out and preserve the quality of the hay.

If a young girl or girls came to the field as visitors to help with the harvesting, the boys would chase them with a sample of hay in their hands. Eventually they would be caught, or allow themselves to be caught, and the hay was rubbed around their faces, which was rather harsh to their tender skin. The boys then had the pleasure of kissing and rolling them in the hay. We used to call it 'making the hay sweet'

At times the women would make the loads of hay, pitched by forks by the men. When the load was finished, ropes were used to keep the load from falling. However, when the woman or women making the load got off the cart, descending to the ground by holding on to the ropes, we could see up their skirts and their bloomers made from flour bags. One could not help but see written across a bottom the name of the brand of flour, 'As You Like It.' Of course these episodes would bring a little humour to the boys, but not raise their expectations too much.

The loaded wagons were taken to the mowhay and unloaded by a hay pole consisting of a soft long pole held aloft by four guy ropes, a swivel arm reaching out with a pulley at each end and a wire rope threaded to a larger pulley at the base of the pole, through which the wire rope was run to a horse attended by a responsible person, going forward to haul the hay from wagon to rick.

It was the normal procedure to have a harvest basket laden with food, usually taken to the fields by the womenfolk, and after the day's work was done, go to the farmhouse kitchen and enjoy a hearty meal with barons of beef and home-made cooking washed down with cider. During the harvest period my mother used to take the hampers, large kettles and food to the fields for our lunch and this used to be quite exciting because we could get together, sit down and have a chat, the horses resting still harnessed to the binder.

Bringing in the harvest was a family event together with the workmen on the farm. We had two workmen full time and a seasonal worker to help at harvest. We all used to gather together in the field and have the harvest picnic. Father used to buy a barrel of cider every year; this was a big thing for us boys, to have a little drop of cider from the barrel. The farmworkers would enjoy a drop of cider with some cheese, pasties and saffron cake. Mother was good at baking saffron cakes. She was also good at making very large pasties and she'd cut them into sections for each worker to have their own section of pasty. Pasties in those days were real pasties, not mince, but chopped beef with chipped potatoes and chopped turnips. She would make other pasties too, apple pasties.

Very large pasties, quite large, perhaps a foot, two feet long would be baked in the clome oven, a type of oven now only seen in museums. It is a hole in the side wall of the hearth lined with bricks and a cast iron door. Filling it with burning wood and hot embers would get it to a certain heat, and to do the baking in this oven the ashes were cleaned out before putting in the bread, cakes or pasties. It was very hard and hot work especially with so many mouths to feed.

My sisters used to come out into the fields and help mum bring out the pasties and food and drinks. They also tried to help sometimes during the harvest season with stooking the sheaves in the field and loading the wagons.

During the winter months a regular seasonal event was threshing the sheaves of corn stored in the ricks into straw and oats. Oats for the horses and cattle, and straw for the winter bedding. With no sheds, everything had to be ricked and thatched with reed or rushes, and sometimes the weather was that bad that the driving rain would penetrate any area that hadn't been adequately thatched. The water used to seep down and ruin tons and tons of sheaves in the rick. We used to feed to the stock sheaves that were grown together with the wet and eventually we would get down to a dry part of the rick and that was put through the thresher.

Bill Weekes the local contractor used to come in with his steam engine and large threshing machine and set up next to the ricks either out in the fields or more usually in the farmyard. There was a set procedure when Bill and his thresher came to thrash our corn. He would usually arrive on the prior evening with his huge steam engine and bulky thresher in tow. He would then get set up for the following day. A second man would stay at the farm for the night. His job was to rise early the next morning to get up steam for the engine. Farmers and labourers would arrive early the next morning from neighbouring farms to help. It required approximately ten men in all, two or three pitching from the rick to the thresher, one cutting open the sheaves, one feeding the thrasher, two to attend to the corn being bagged and hauled on one's shoulder to be carried to the barn, and two working on the straw and chaff. They had to have their lunch brought to the field or to the farmyard. Everyone was very busy at threshing time. The lunch and supper was quite an occasion when the characters assembled and began to discuss events among themselves. The help we received from neighbours was later reciprocated by us helping them in turn with their threshing. There was no payment; neighbours in our community helped each other at threshing time. As a teenager I used to help in carrying large sacks of oats from the thresher to the barn on my back, up the barn steps, tip the bags out in the barn and then back to collect the next bag and these were two hundredweight bags. My dear old legs, I've still got them but how I managed those steps I shall never know. I suppose I had plenty of practice, father used to send me up to the railway station with horse and cart to load up maize meal, two hundredweight West of England sacks, I still remember them, they were big and took some handling.

I WOULD think it was 1941, I was about 21 and my father bought this tractor for £115, a standard Fortune with iron wheels. He used to keep the tractor in the shed and that used to infuriate me because I wanted to drive it. Once you drove the tractor and had done your day's work, you parked the tractor in the shed, turned off the engine and that was the end of it. No grooming, no feeding, nothing more to do. It used to infuriate me when father used to say: 'William, you take those horses, go up in the field and plough, do what you have to do'. The reason was that he used to breed shire horses and had me and my brother get them fit for the chains and the shafts.He'd have a man come and look around the horses and he would sell them and we'd have to train up another lot of young horses. We always had the old nags, they were always with us, the old nags we called them but actually father was rather proud of his well-schooled young draught horses. We used to bring on the young stock, he would sell them off and keep the tractor in the shed. Brother and I were exasperated at this, we wanted rid of the horses and get on with the modern way. On the tractor you could go out and do two or three acres a day, with the horses you would be struggling to get through an acre a day.

I was receiving some instruction with this new high-wheeled Fortune standard tractor from the tractor dealer, you pushed out the clutch, and you pushed the clutch even further to use the brake. Take your foot off, away goes the tractor, you wouldn't if you didn't put it in neutral, which I didn't know. 'Fall in young man, get off the tractor.' He told me how to stop it because I had not driven a tractor before. 'When you want to stop put your foot down on that,' I held my foot down there for a while and he was there standing around behind. 'Come on there, off you get and help me. Of course, off came my foot from the clutch and away goes the tractor. By the time I regained control the tractor was about to enter the hedge, anyway that was the first experience I ever had of driving a tractor.

The tractor was eventually brought on to the farm but kept in the shed and, to my disgust, the horse still had its place during my father's time, the reason being that the horse ate what was produced on the farm and young horses were broken in to do farm work and eventually sold to bring in additional capital. I see the logic but I didn't keep to it when I became more involved. However modern machinery was essential but financing it was a different position and one had to compromise.

To start the iron wheeled tractor we had to hand crank the engine, petrol start initially, then turn over to TVO, tractor vapouring oil. To stop the tractor one brake and clutch foot pedal was used. The tractor had to have some machinery attached behind it if the tractor was to be of any use, and this meant a complete re-organising of the farm implements. Machines for use with tractors were much improved and wider in scope than the original horse machines. They included a hay cutting machine, fielder and turner, baler and a host of other machines suitable for the various work in their seasons. Also it entailed extra capital, hence a periodic visit to (we hoped) a friendly bank manager.

The machinery agents during those early days had a bonanza because during those days of change farmers generally were obliged to mechanise their farms to produce a lot more food for the war effort. Pre-war and during the war we were jointly farming Stone Farm and Fentrigan Farm with a distance between them of about fifteen miles, so transport was important. There were times when we used horses either by riding or by carriage to go between the two farms and later on we used tractors. I remember on one occasion near Camelford driving the tractor back from Stone when it overheated and was running short of water. I called into a farmhouse by the road and near a quarry. I knocked loudly several times on the open door; there was no answer. I shouted: 'Hello is anyone about?' still no answer so I ventured inside still calling loudly: 'Anyone at home?' I saw a woman in the kitchen and I walked right up to her before she noticed me. I gave her quite a fright. She was stone deaf. I did get some water for the tractor eventually from the farmer outside in the farmyard but he charged me sixpence. I didn't think much of him for charging me for water.

With a limited amount of cash available we were in desperate need of some basic farm machinery. A priority was a trailer to tow behind the recently acquired tractor. From Mr Luckhurst of Beals Mill near Kelly Bray we bought an old lorry chassis and the chassis was modified into a trailer by Bert Wilton of Smiths Garage, Launceston, who went to Beals Mill with me to do the necessary work. We towed the chassis home and in my spare time I succeeded in making the trailer floor. Later on I bought from Cecil Kelly's Bridge Farm sale a set of grass harrows and a tractor converted grass mower. We now had the basics of some mechanisation on the farm. We were obliged to plough up a large acreage whereas before the war only a small acreage was under the plough.

This renewing of the old worn-out pastures for modern methods certainly improved the output and with much scientific work done on cereal and grass research helped to a considerable extent to produce the food that we were expected to for the war effort. War Agricultural Committee representatives would dictate what fields had to be ploughed and planted to cereals. Some linseed, which we found difficult to harvest and also growing flax that was like wire to cut. Progress since those days has been truly exciting and for one to have lived and worked in those Victorian-type days and then adapt and transform one's views to modern methods was a major change for agriculture and for farmers like myself.

Dad wanted to keep the horses. He enjoyed it I think and it was necessary this bringing on of young horses. I can see the logic, money was tight and he didn't want to go spending a lot of money on fuel when the farm had hay, straw, oats for the horses, plus a little labour of course, which was cheap very cheap. Many a time especially during harvest time, he'd say: 'William, you take that turnip hoe and go up in the field and hoe those mangles and turnips for stock'. The sun would be shining, the weeds would be growing, you would do a bit with the workmen, two or three of us up there in the sunshine. In the afternoon we would go out and try to turn this hay in the field. Never had a hay turner, had a horse rake yes, he invested in a horse rake but we had to turn the hay by hand

Mother used to get mad with him at times, especially at harvest time, he was so set in his ways, the weather had to be right, the conditions had to be just so before he would really get moving with the harvest, mother had a lot more get up and go in her and she would sometimes back us up in trying to get dad to see the error of his ways. For example where was the logic in going up in the field and using the turnip hoe when we had hay lying in the field ready to be harvested?

Many a time I've been out on the mower at three, four, five-o-clock in the morning. I would take fresh horses, go out in the fields, harness the mower, and start mowing the grass with the horses early in the mornings, before the sun really came up high. Summer months in the daytime we had to go out and work in the fields and the horses used to rest a bit through the day.

It was a rare occasion to be privileged to see a motor car. At an early age of approximately 14 years I was sent off to the field of eight acres called Grey Down, with two horses harnessed for the plough. It was considered that a day's ploughing would do an acre, that is if your horses were well groomed, fed and fit. Following the plough, walking in the furrows, having the control of the horses by long rein, occasionally using the long rein rope to speed them along by swishing the rope to the horse's side, I have had many a bruised rib from the plough handles through the plough bouncing off large rocks hidden beneath the surface. In retrospect compared to the modern mechanised method there was a great satisfaction to be had in ploughing with horses but I did not appreciate it at that time, as it was a steady and slow process, and what was not done today would be done tomorrow. I well remember stopping the horses upon hearing a motor car, running as fast as I could to the roadside hedge and tearing through the thicket, being scratched in the process, just to see a car passing by, usually owned either by a doctor or a vet, as the average family did not or could ill afford a motor car. This of course was news to tell others at home and after our day's work following the plough I would ride one horse and lead the other home to the farmyard pond for a drink before stabling, grooming and feeding. The horses always had first priority and after they were settled, fed and bedded down for the night it would be my turn to have a well-earned meal.

There was a lot more wildlife about in those days and especially early in the morning. Skylarks, partridges, hares, and the peewits and lapwings used to get really excited if you were cultivating a field where they had a nest. You wouldn't see the eggs, they are the same colour as the soil, but tiny chicks would be running about.Winter months also involved work in the fields pulling mangels and cutting kale by hand and loading on to a cart. I used to suffer terribly on my hands from chaps from the fine dust from grooming horses.

MY MUM used to make butter and cream and take eggs to sell at market in Launceston by horse and trap, sometimes from the station, and sometimes she would go all the way to Launceston by horse and trap. On one particular occasion Farmer Uglow next door cut down some wood and left it lying in the lane. The trap wheel caught in a large stick and as we were going along the lane, sitting up above, mum and me, the trap turned upside down and threw the lot out into the mud. I ran into my dad and I could never understand why he didn't run, he didn't make any effort to go any faster, I was saying: 'Quick, quick, mum's in trouble with the horses, upside down and everything!' and 'Oh, oh, all right,' he said. He walked a bit faster but he didn't run and I couldn't understand it. Anyway when he got out there mum had pulled herself out of the tangle and got herself sorted out a bit, but the disappointing thing was that I didn't have a chance to go Launceston. That was a disappointment for me as a lad of six or seven as mother didn't usually take children along with her when she went to Launceston

There were other trips, once or twice a year mother would get a hamper made up and take us to the beach in the horse and trap, and I used to become quite excited when I got over the hill looking down on to the beach at Crackington Haven. I couldn't get there quick enough. It was quite an experience. I believe I went there with my brother Richard as my sisters weren't old enough. At one time when we were going there I remember the workmen building the bridge at Trengune. It was a ford, and I remember these pillars and the men there. I was not very old, about four or five years old. I do remember those trips to the seaside. I couldn't swim; I just paddled about a bit and played with the sand. It was only for an hour or two but it was like having a great day out.

Every year before Christmas dad used to go to Plymouth with poultry. He would leave the farm about two o'clock in the morning, with the dead poultry packed in tea chests, he used to pal up with his dad at Kyrse because he also used to rear ducks and geese for the Christmas market

The pair of them took a horse and wagon in the dark, loaded with poultry, to get to Kelly Bray station, near Callington to catch the early morning train to Plymouth. Dad had stabling arranged at Kelly Bray and he would load the train and go on to Plymouth. The station at Plymouth would arrange for his load of tea chests to be taken to the market and Mrs Edwards, Mr Weeks and some other butchers and dealers would be there waiting for the delivery of Mr Grigg's poultry. Before making the return journey dad used to buy mum a present, for she'd done the rearing of the poultry, and she used to work very hard. Always a handbag, every year he'd buy mum a handbag.

At the age of 55 he had a heart attack while on his annual trip to Plymouth with the Christmas poultry. He was very ill for many months and lived a further ten years until 1955. My dad's pleasure in looking back was his family, myself, elder brother Richard, Adelaide, my eldest sister, Henrietta (Betty), my middle sister and Sylvia, the younger sister. My mum was a very active woman and completely different from my father's very steady character. During the summer she used to rear a large number of geese, ducks, turkeys and chicken by using the hens, when they became broody, to hatch them out. Any addled eggs were put aside. Throwing these rotten eggs at each other, I caught my brother Richard directly in the face. The egg, with its horrible smell on being smashed, sent him crying to mum, who did the necessary cleaning up. Being hesitant as to my next move, on getting reasonably close to my victim, I was rewarded with a smile from her. When quite small I would chase a small gosling with a stick, kill it and bring it to show my mother, saying, 'Another gosling dead mummy.' She became suspicious of why they were dying so quickly and watched my movements, I was caught in the act and there were no more dead goslings.

To rear these birds for the Christmas market was a painstaking and laborious process and entailed a lot of hard work. The hens would shelter the small birds against the elements; foxes were a source of danger. Approximately a fortnight before Christmas extra staff would be brought in to hand pluck these birds, in a room adjoining the farmhouse, sitting around on chairs and forms, six to eight people all plucking, and feathers building up around us. The plucked birds were then collected by the ladies present, drawn and laid out ready for the market, being put on to slate slabs to cool off in a large dairy.

Father, having packed the poultry in tea chests, all with greaseproof paper and loaded them on to wagons, took them to Kelly Bray Station for the Plymouth market. When lorries became available we had the poultry collected from the farm and taken direct to the Plymouth shops. This was discontinued after 1942-3, Plymouth being hit by the German bombs, and one could no longer get established, and I was not interested in carrying on the business.

The butcher, Jack Ridgeman, I remember as tall with a fresh complexion and ginger hair, coming every week to the farm with the horse and butcher's cart with the beef and other meats. My mum would meet him with a large oval plate that was filled with a week's supply of meats. Once every month a call was made by the grocery man to take the orders for the month's supply of flour bought by the sack, sugar and rock salt, various currants, raisins and other necessaries used for home cooking. This was delivered some days after the order was given, and sufficient for one month's supply. During the winter months there was always the risk of being cut off by snowdrifts in the farm drive.

Cooking was done in the clome oven, including pasties, bread, cakes, puddings and other treats. The hams and pig's shoulders were home-cured and had a lovely flavour. The chickens, especially the Indian Gam breed, were plump with large breasts and legs, bred especially for the table.

In those days even the vegetables had a special flavour not found today. Livestock must have time to mature before being killed, to obtain the best flavour. Unfortunately modern methods spoil the flavour of the product. It was all home cooking. I never remember seeing a tin opener or any food out of a tin. The garden was quite large and was used for growing vegetables, rhubarb, onions, potatoes etc. We grew a few acres of potatoes for our own use and animal use in the fields; cabbages, mangolds, turnips, rape etc.

I recall going to catch the train at Treneglos station with my mother. She was a wonderful horsewoman; she had a hackney and trap. Coming up to the station but still some distance from it many times I remember the horse had a sixth sense and he used to put the steam on to get to the train on time. We would get to the station, train would then be pulling in, off the trap, jump on the train and into Launceston, and Mr Rowe, the blacksmith, used to take the trap and the horse into his stables there till we came back in the afternoon.

One day mum and Mrs Evans, a lady that used to help my mother, were sitting up in the trap, crossing the railway bridge above Tresmeer station when for some reason the horse decided he wanted to go in reverse, so into reverse they all went and the trap was pushed back against the bridge parapet and my mum and Mrs Evans found themselves looking down on the engine below. It was quite scary as there was quite a drop on to the railway lines below.

Mother was some proud of her special hackney and rallye trap. He was a good horse and it was very much a source of pride and status as to who could have the best trap in the district. I remember that father some years later took this hackney to Reading horse sale and sold it, I can't remember why, perhaps money was tight anyhow we replaced with another horse called Twinkle who had springholt. We had to have a horse for transport; we only ever had one horse.

My job was to get up every morning and go out into the field to try and catch this damned Twinkle who didn't want to be caught. I used to get so fed up with it, what a job every morning, catching this horse for one of my sisters to ride to Tresmeer Station to catch a train to Launceston and then walk the quarter mile to the convent school. Back again every evening, that was the round trip.

LOOKING BACK

My three younger sisters all went at first to the same village school as me, but Adelaide and Betty, the two eldest, went to the local convent as day pupils when they were old enough. For some reason that I can't remember, Sylvia the youngest didn't go to St Joseph's Convent in Launceston. We were self sufficient in most respects but cash had to be found to pay the fees for Adelaide and Betty.

I would have loved to have gone to a private school, I dearly wanted to go, other children from other families went to the local grammar school at Launceston College but my parents couldn't afford it. My father wanted me home to work and my brother Richard too. My mum and dad were devoted parents, always wanting what was best for their five children and they worked hard to give us what they could, but they didn't understand then that there might have been another life out there for Richard and me, other than farming. Education was the key to that other life but for my brother and I, it was leave school at thirteen and come home on the farm. I would have loved to have stayed on at school, in fact my Aunt Adelaide at Stone desperately wanted me to come down and live with her and she would have sent me at her expense to a private school in Bodmin.

Richard, Betty, Adelaide, Me at Fentrigan 1929

My life would have possibly been so different had my parents allowed it, but we were a united family. We grew up as a family of five children; one child didn't go off to private school and leave the others at home scraping the mud. We all had to do the same thing. It probably wasn't the right decision that was made but that was my destiny then, home to work! My formal schooling was all over at the tender age of thirteen.

There was an occasion related to me by the local postman who saw my mum one day in Launceston, shopping. She had to hurry to catch the train at the station, which was about a mile down the road, and she left the shop without paying. Of course the attendant at the shop chased her, caught her eventually and tapped her on the shoulder: 'Hey, you haven't paid your bill.' The postman told me that mother was so apologetic, he could see it was very embarrassing for her. She was in a hurry, that was my mum, so much to do, so little time, quite excitable, yes, but a worker, no doubt about that. She had a quick temper but it didn't last.

She was quite artistic in her own way; she was quite accomplished at drawing, vases of flowers, faces and things like that. As a child she and her sister had to do their morning chores at the house and then after lunch they liked to sit down and do needlework or painting. Her mother was a very efficient person, and it came through to my mother too.

I sometimes think, dare I say it, my mother married beneath her in marrying my dad. My mum's side, the Weary family, was more enlightened than the Grigg family was. Of course, coming from an area like St Mabyn where nature deals a kinder and more bountiful hand may have had something to do with it. Fentrigan Farm where the Griggs have lived for hundreds of years is hard country, more unforgiving where the soil is thinner and trees are fewer

I've often thought how different, challenging, even shocking it must have been to my mother, when as a relatively young woman with two boys of six and two, she and her husband took on the then derelict Fentrigan. By all accounts my great uncle had left it in such a terrible state that the Duchy of Cornwall was only too glad to sell it to my father. Coming to Fentrigan must have given them both pause for thought, but they both buckled down to it, they farmed the land, they made it support them and their family. I know my mother knew that life would never have been quite so hard for her if she had never come to Fentrigan.

Looking back, in those days times were hard and the farm money was short. There was no time for leisure, only long hours of work, with no pay, my dad did not allow us to get involved in sport because of possibly being hurt. It is not good to be over-protected because some time you are going to bust out. This is what happened to me later. He loved his family and looking back one sees his wisdom (or lack of it).

On Sundays his pleasure was to get the family around the American Organ, mum playing some hymns, dad the violin, and we children singing. I must say that I did not cherish the idea but looking back on it I now realise the true value of family life. He was a regular attender at our parish church, and paraded us along to the Sunday School, a distance of two miles. My mum would organise whist drives and other social events for the church. The decorating of the church and upkeep of the churchyard was a labour of love from local people.

An annual trip that I used to hate was driving all the sheep to his old farm at Kyrse to be dipped, about five miles. Horse and cart would pick up the stragglers. The road was narrow and long but this job did not last too long, thank goodness. In later years we built our own sheep dip and this annual event was one that I was glad to see the back off. Going to visit my grandfather at Kyrse Farm one day, he not being there, I returned with my bicycle fitted with a gas front light along the narrow lanes when in the darkness a horse and trap appeared and, silhouetted against the sky, a person sitting up in the trap. I had to suddenly get out of the way and fell into the hedge. Behind the trap were a lot of bushes being dragged along the road, taking up the full width of the lane. Not having any lights on a horse and trap I suppose was not unusual. On my arrival back home I reported my experience to my dad and he had no hesitation as to the identity of the fellow in question. It was my grandfather returning from his other farm at Trebreak with his load of firewood trailing behind. Firewood was in very short supply at Fentrigan so Trebreak was a convenient but distant source of supply. Cutting and hauling trees there from near the river to the road was bad enough but to get it to our farm on horse drawn fully laden wagons was no mean effort. Father would say to us boys at breakfast on a wintry morning before setting off to haul wood, 'Where you are going today have a good meal as you will find the cupboards are high.'

I remember the road on a particular day was frozen over with ice. Going up this very steep hill, two horses hauling the wagon loaded with wood could not make it and they were struggling to stay on their feet. Horses and wagon could no longer move forward. Sliding back and gathering speed, we eventually hit the hedge on a sharp bend and came to a stop. It was a very frightening experience and we should never have attempted such a disastrous climb. I recall how the horse's legs were torn and bleeding but fortunately no serious damage. We eventually got moving again but not before the load was made lighter.

I remember my dad, selling some sheep at our local market at Hallworthy to Mr Tom Spettigue, who then asked me to drive them to his farm at Canworthy Water. I was about seven to eight years old, the farm about three to four miles away. He gave me sixpence and I felt like a millionaire and was very happy to do it

I remember a particular Sunday day out with my parents, driving to Warleggan with mum, dad and Reverend Jenkins to Trevedda tin mine, before calling at Warleggan Church. On entering the church gate we were greeted by the vicar a Reverend Densham, the organist and churchwarden. Reverend Densham was so enthusiastic to meet us; a rather tall man dressed in a long surplice, giving the impression to me of being a strange sort of man. The church was small with a cold atmosphere and, having been shown around and the history of the church being explained, he insisted that we go to the rectory and be shown over the grounds. Leaving the compound of the church we proceeded to the rectory entrance.

On arriving at the gate we were confronted by a ten-foot high wire fence, topped by barbed wire, and ten to fifteen dogs of all shapes and sizes. With a bundle of keys, from which I found it difficult to see how he could pick out the correct keys for that particular gate, he opened up and we entered with great trepidation. The dogs were very inquisitive, some of them did bark but they all had a good sniff and he reassured us that all was well. They eventually dispersed and he proceeded to show us the grounds. He was in the process of making a play area for children, with all sorts of weird and strange scenes. At the rectory, he was in the process of building a veranda. We were all given a hearty invitation to come when it was completed.

Near Warleggan is Trevedda Tin Mine Farm which was farmed by my mum's uncle Tom

Worden, who incidentally was asked by the authorities to shoot all the dogs at the rectory when the Reverend died some years later. My mum's grandfather, Mr Worden, used to work at the mine and by horse and wagon took the tin to Par Docks for export.

I was about 18 years of age when dad and mum invited to tea my Aunt Mary of about 45 years and her new husband Henry of about 50 years. Aunt Mary was my dad's eldest sister, very proper and with a strong Methodist streak. Uncle Henry Turner was from a local farming family, of the same type of background, a tall well-built, well-groomed man. I had never met him before and I thought how funny his ways were, softly spoken and at almost every few words he would say to me, 'Yes Willie dear.' Before tea, which was for all the family including Ziebelt (Zip), the German POW, there were a few minutes to show him around the farm buildings. On climbing the ladder to get some hay to feed the calves, I heard a very loud belch. I made a hurried retreat down the ladder, thinking that something had upset the dog. The dog seemed perfectly normal, and then again another volcanic outburst. My uncle, turning sharply around and holding his chest, seemed as though he was in great pain. I inquired of his welfare, he assured me he was all right and thanked me for my concern, not once but several times. 'You see, Willie dear, it's my heart.' (He lived to be a very old man).

This was my introduction to my new uncle; I found it highly amusing sitting at our family table, dad, my sisters, Zip and myself. Uncle Henry and my mum sat together, Aunt Mary next to her. During that time, Uncle Henry would hold on to my mum's arm and say to her: 'Dear sister, yes, dear sister', spoken in very soft and endearing terms. This continued for a while and before we had finished our meal, I thought a bit of fun would not be amiss. Getting up and going to uncle Henry with an unopened packet of cigarettes, I offered him one, knowing full well he would refuse. 'You see Willie, I don't smoke. Thank you ever so much for your kindness in offering. You see, dear Willie I like sweets instead.' Having retreated to my seat, again hearing his 'dear sister' outburst, I asked my dad to watch out or we might be losing our mum. His reply was quite spontaneous: 'I am not a naughty man, Willie.' This outburst was received by all of as very humorous and we all had a good laugh.

EDGAR Dawe died quite recently, and a very popular man he was. He worked as a farm labourer for my dad for several years. He had the habit of saying to me: 'I bet your dad's scoots were shining when you were born.' Scoots are the metal part of the boots, the toe and heel caps. It was his way of saying that my dad must have been mightily proud the day I was born. One day I had the opportunity of getting my own back. Dawe was working on the laying of an hedge I walked up to him, picked up one of his feet, dropped it back, and then picked up the other one. 'What the hell's going on?' he said. I said: 'I'm just checking that your scoots are shining.' He had very recently that same week had a son or daughter born.

A farm labourer wages at that time in 1935 was about thirty shillings a week. Money was scarce and sometimes dad had difficulty paying the wages and I remember one time taking young ewes to Holsworthy market. They didn't sell for a lot and at other times he would have brought them home again but he had to sell them to have the money to pay the wages. We had two full-time labourers Edgar and Bill Parnall. Good men they were, local village men, married in their forties and fifties with families to support. Alf Nicholls, a simple-minded single farm labourer, worked for us for some years until he became involved with a local family, who egged him on to get married to one of their own family. I cannot exactly recall the details but I remember my father becoming involved and not long after he left our employ. I remember Alf receiving in the post one morning a hundred or so wedding invitation cards addressed to him

I remember during the harvesting of the corn that the front horse pulling the wagon laden with sheaves of corn would be unhitched, to be rested. I begged Alf to let me ride the unhitched horse. He sat me on the back of this young, inexperienced horse and with this boy rider with the leathers and chains swinging, it moved off and started a trot then a gallop, with me holding tight to the harness, the chains swinging wildly, hitting the horse's belly. It made me quite scared. I wanted to jump off while in full gallop but was afraid of being caught up in the chains and dragged along. However I stayed with the horse and we arrived at the stable door. My dad came along and gave me a boot on the backside and a good lecture. When Alf Nicholls came into the farmyard with the shaft horse and wagon loaded with corn Dad gave the same treatment to him.

At age fourteen I had to leave school to work on the farm, one day I had to harness up three horses and was sent to the field to do the ploughing with a Climax type single furrow plough. On this occasion the field was very wet and the fore-ends were quite sodden. I had great difficulty in handling three strong horses, especially when turning at the fore-ends. Wearing hobnail boots with leather leggings, corduroy breeches with button-in linens, one had a very difficult manoeuvre to get the plough back into place at the ends, mud and slurry halfway up your legs, the plough running to land making pigs troughs, as we called it. For three horses it required a triple whipstrees, three single whipstrees and a lot of knowledge as to how to handle all these reins. I was only a growing boy, I sweated, my nose bled and I was frustrated, being almost afraid to unharness and return.

On another occasion I had to take a horse and cart and shovel to the bottom part of a field called 'Long Park'. The earth over the years had built up against the lower hedge of the field and I was asked to take the earth by cart to the top part of the same field. This job was never-ending, but my father soon tired of it, as I certainly did.

Edgar Dawe worked for us mostly during the war years. He was well respected. Having worked late one corn harvesting day, the weather changing to rain, we decided to clear the sheaves from the field. Leaving Dawe at about ten o'clock one night I roped down and proceeded to the farmyard with the horse and laden wagon. On arriving my job was to unharness the mare and muck out the stable. She had a young foal and if the foal sucked in sweated milk it could have disastrous results. However I let the mare cool down and went for a well-earned meal. Having finished my meal at about midnight I had to put the mare with her foal in the field about half a mile from the farm. This done, I closed the gate and turned for home. I saw someone approaching in the dark shadows. Getting nearer, I was surprised to see Edgar Dawe who I had left about two hours previously in the field. 'Bloody well lost myself. Got pixie-led,' he said. 'Oh dear,' I said trying not to laugh. 'You should have been home two hours ago.' He had become confused and disorientated and had spent the last few hours walking in circles in the dark trying to find his way home. He knew the farm but he put it down to the mischievous pixies.

Once when working in a cornfield at the lower part of the farm, trying to clear all the sheaves in the final load, we got them all on and before the ropes could be put over the load it started to slip on the side of the hill and half the load came off. Dad watched this performance from an adjoining field; he was doing some second raking with the horse and rake. He stopped his horse, dismounted from the rake and, leaving the horse, came to where we were, Edgar and I, not saying much. His remarks were very much to the point and no questions asked. 'William, you take in that remaining half load, unload it by yourself, come back here and reload what has fallen off and take it to the rick by yourself.' And then to Dawe he said 'Go down in Lower Long Park, turn the sheaves that need turning and stook the sheaves in the rest of the field.' My father's orders were not to be questioned and I did as I was told.

SOMETIMES when staying at Stone farm in my holidays I would help in driving cattle from various forms to Wadebridge market. There would be about three or four of us doing the droving and each would have brought along some cattle from their own farm. I would be taking some of my aunt's cattle to market and altogether there might be ten or fifteen cattle in total. I remember when we reached near Wadebridge one bullock was a bit wild and jumped the fence into the river Camel, a tidal river and rather deep in this part near the bridge. So we had this bullock swimming across the river and all you could see was his nostrils, blowing water. It was quite funny to us as this fellow called Bill who worked for Farmer Davey, whose bullock it was, began to get quite agitated thinking the bullock would drown. Bill got down on his knees and prayed, holding his stick up in the air. Anyhow his prayers were answered, for no sooner had we stopped laughing and Bill had stopped praying than the bullock who was now halfway across the river turned and came back again.

COUNTRY CHARACTERS

THE FARM being mainly down to grassland and with numerous banks and hedges was a wonderful breeding ground for rabbits. We had them by the thousands. A serious problem was how to keep them under control.

Rabbits were a sensitive issue with some of the local trappers. They bought the rabbits from various farmers and trapping was an opportunity to earn a useful living. Obviously the trappers would never attempt to catch too many, but left sufficient for breeding purposes. The blacksmith who was our trapper used to buy the rabbits from my father, although when my brother and I took over more of the farming just before the war we got fed up with the blacksmith. He wouldn't catch the rabbits like he should, so Dick and I decided to catch them ourselves and we got quite a little enterprise going, regularly sending rabbits to Smithfield market. Rabbit was a very popular food in those days and several farmers and trappers would send rabbits by train to Smithfield.

The local trappers, the Bolts for instance, didn't like the idea of what we were doing one bit, they hated the idea of anybody taking away their livelihood. The rabbits became such a terrible problem on the farm that large areas of crops were being destroyed. We used the gin trap (now illegal); it helped somewhat in controlling numbers but being such prolific breeders they could not be kept under control. The best method was by lurcher and lamp. In the early part of the war we had a fantastic lurcher dog and using two six volt car batteries and an old Daimler car headlight we did quite well. The best nights were when it was windy and dry. Numerous rabbits would be out in the small fields and you would pick out a rabbit in the strong light beam, the rabbit would crouch, and the dog used to go around the beam and then when he got near the rabbit he'd pounce, the rabbit of course was still crouched down, frightened by the light, and not knowing about the dog that was about to pick him up and carry back to us. Off would go the light, dog delivers the rabbit, break its neck, switch the light on again, pick out the next rabbit, dog would not follow the beam but go outside the beam, pick up another rabbit, bring him back, same process. One night we caught fifty rabbits. We also used to take our fantastic lurcher down to our other farm at St Maybn and after a night of rabbiting and having left the dog there I was surprised the following day when the dog returned of its own accord the fifteen miles back to Fentrigan.

I recollect a neighbouring farmer called Jim Statton at Tredarrup who did a lot of trapping and made a regular annual setting of gin traps on a boundary hedge belonging jointly to us. He, over several years, would lay his traps and have a very big catch. My brother Dick and I decided as teenagers that we should get in on this annual harvest and one year we beat him to it and got there first. To make matters worse for him we dragged a rag soaked in paraffin on his side of the hedge thereby stopping the rabbits using the holes on his side. The rabbits did not like the smell of paraffin and would all come out on our side and we would catch them with lamp and lurcher or with gins traps. When he realised the extent of his loss he became very annoyed and suffered a definite loss of face. His wife Mabel was some furious, she came into see my mother, 'rabbits was their living, we were not welcome'. We however had done nothing wrong and continued the following year.

We beat them to it that year as well and used the paraffin trick again.

There were also professional trappers and poachers who made a full-time living out of trapping rabbits and selling the skins and fur. I remember a fellow called Bill, he would clean a hedge out overnight. He would put his dog over the hedge to work one side and Bill would work the other side with his nets and ferrets. In goes the ferret; rabbits hear the noise of the ferret and bolt either into the nets or to the dog waiting at the open hole the other side, all other holes having been stopped. If the dog grabbed he would silently bring the rabbit over to drop at Bill's feet for despatch. The particular thing about Bill was that there was no noise at all, the peace and quiet of the dog one side, picking up the rabbit, dropping it back at Bill's feet and back again, waiting for the next rabbit and the ferret in the burrow quietly going about his business of driving out the rabbits was a highly effective and quiet natural killing machine.

Sometimes Bill would work a hedge where he had not been invited. Rabbits were sometimes the only source of income for many trappers and tempers would rise if it were known that a trapper had been working hedges that were normally controlled by the farmer or another rabbit man. There was one particular occasion the police stopped him. Bill was supposed to have been out poaching salmon that night but when the constable asked him to empty out his bag instead of a salmon to the constable's surprise old boots, shoes and other bits of material were displayed. It was Bill's lucky night

There are relatively very few rabbits on the farm today compared to pre-myxamatosis days. Indeed there are fewer rabbits everywhere. The rabbit infestation was solved on my farm by two main factors, hedgerow removal and introduction of myxamatosis. When I took over the farming in 1946 the fields were small and I decided to bulldoze a number of hedges and make the fields into large economic units; the old six-foot wide gateways with their granite posts were wide enough for horse-drawn implements but I wanted to mechanise, become more efficient and use tractor-drawn machinery. Going to a farm sale and buying a tractor drawn ring roller gave me no choice and forced me to make the gateways to at least ten feet as I had bought a roller this wide at the sale.

Standing on a bank one beautiful sunny spring evening also helped motivate me to tackle the rabbit problem. The fields literally moved with my sudden presence on the bank. The rabbits gave their warning by showing their white tails and rushed to their burrows but had to queue up to get inside. Shortly afterwards a report in the local paper said myxomatosis was in the Lerryn area near Lostwithiel. My friend Tommy Dinniss and I went by prior arrangement one night to a pub at Lerryn to meet a farmer who could help us. I had had a fair bit to drink so when the time came to go and catch these infected rabbits I sat and watched from the middle of the field whilst Tommy and this farmer using a dog and lamp collected approximately six live rabbits. Back at Fentrigan we mixed them with a number of other healthy rabbits that we stole from the blacksmith's gin traps and held them in tea chests for a few days before distributing them around the farm. Nothing happened for a fortnight but the myxie eventully took hold and spread like wildfire. The numbers dying were so many that the dying rabbits would go to the boundary road (a council road) but not any further and die in the road. The road was so full of flesh that council workmen used to come and try to clean the road up. Myxamatosis caused terrible suffering and distress but it cleaned them out completely. Farmers, including myself, who introduced myxomatosis into the area were very unpopular with the trappers and their families. It was also amazing how many farmers came to the farm to collect these rabbits, the object being to spread the disease, but they did not want to be seen.

I HAD a cow that had recently given birth to a calf and not having fully discharged the placenta became ill after some days. Having tried unsuccessfully to solve it by tying an old boot to the exterior hanging part of the placenta, I was obliged to call a veterinary surgeon, young Mr Richardson from Wadebridge. He was well spoken with a mass of ginger coloured hair, aged about twenty five. He arrived and gave her a thorough inspection, implying that there was not much he could do with her except to drench her with a gallon of ale to help with her loss of appetite. He said to me, 'Sonny, go and see Cyril Levi and get a gallon of ale.' Levi was the publican at our village pub in St Mabyn.

I gathered together sufficient money for the ale and proceeded with my bicycle to call at the pub approximately one mile away. On arrival I was rather apprehensive and nervous as I was only about 15-16 years of age, I plucked up enough courage to knock on the door. 'Come in,' in a loud husky voice. I entered and was given a look from the characters within, which made me feel quite embarrassed. I managed to ask, ' Please can I have a gallon of ale?' This was an unusual request. There was a silence throughout. Levi, being a short and lively man, with a quick glance at his locals, asked: 'What sort of ale do you want sonny. ?' 'Well, you see,' says I, 'I have a cow which is sick and the vet advised me to come here to get a gallon of ale.' 'Whatever for?' chipped in another. 'She has lost her appetite and the ale should help her to recover,' say I. This caused quite a stir within the pub and there was a general discussion throughout as to which brand of beer would be most suitable. Frankie Menheniot (whom I got to know later) was a local cattle dealer and was a regular at the local. They at first tried to establish who I was and where I came from. Having found out my identity they then began to discuss among themselves as to the best beer for the unfortunate animal. I recall how very serious and alarmed they were, but listening to the conversations between the customers I came to the conclusion that it was a big joke. It was at last agreed which was the best ale, and having paid a few pence I went on my way.

A YEAR or two after the above event I went to Wadebridge market to buy a cow. Being young and not experienced in the finer points of dairy farming I ended up buying a cow for the exorbitant price of fifteen pounds. She had a massive great udder, teats almost touching the ground, which I found out later from others keen to offer their advice was because she had a dropped udder and had suffered mastitis in one of her quarters. She was an old cow and fifteen pounds in those days was a lot of money especially to me as I didn't have a lot and as I was trying to get started with a small milking herd of five or six cows which I milked by hand. I was determined to persevere with this cow and make a go of it. I milked her out for twelve months or more and took her back to Wadebridge market where I sold her for about the same price.

Life wasn't entirely work and I decided to join the local church bellringers. On entering the belfry a group of ringers was waiting for me. 'The bell is set'; the leader told me. My brother had previously done some ringing and they thought that I was him.'Get set, pull in your turn', was the order. Not having pulled a bell in my life before, I gave the rope a pull, resulting in yards of slack rope around me. Gathering this rope, eventually it stopped and I, holding tight to the rope, was hauled up the belfry by the weight of the bell swinging about. Looking down at the others, who were confused with my approach to ringing, I held on to the rope and started to descend to the floor, the end result was me being taken back up again, this time not so far, until eventually the bell lay in its correct position. This was a tenor bell; being 'set' means that it is upside down.

On the farm the pigs were dying, vets came and did an autopsy, and were not too sure whether it was erysipelas or swine fever. The police were informed and a restriction order placed on the farm whereby no movement of pigs was allowed, and anyone entering the premises had to dip their footwear in a disinfectant bath situated at the entrance. We were given a permit to slaughter all the pigs that appeared healthy. A butcher, Martin from Launceston, came with his two sons and slaughtered, cleaned and dressed a large number. Prior to their removal the Ministry of Food had to be notified, so speaking to an official at the other end of the telephone from a local kiosk, being my first telephone call, he asked me if they were fit for human consumption. My reply to him was 'No, they are not suffering from human consumption,' upon which my brother snatched the phone from me to put matters right.

MY FIRST experience of listening to the wireless was the abdication speech of Edward VII at Billy Jimmy's house, a neighbouring elderly carpenter whose vocabulary was unfortunate, especially when he was upset. My brother and I saved enough money to purchase our first wireless, a Philco with wet batteries that had to be periodically charged by our local garage. It was such a novelty and very much appreciated.

My first bicycle was earned out of the pennies I struggled to save, taking about two years, and bought from our local agent, a blacksmith, for about six pounds. It was such a treasure after such a long wait that it was part of my life. I was about 14-15 years old at the time. I refused to go anywhere by car and would much rather go by my bicycle, sometimes to the farm at St Mabyn fifteen miles away. It was always kept polished and clean and reserved only for myself. Cycling was my choice for several years. I remember cycling homeward merrily along at the top end of Fore Street, Bodmin, one Saturday evening after going to the cinema with my friend Ken Simcock. As I rode my dropped handlebar machine I sang: 'It's a sin to tell a lie, I love you, yes I do, I love you', as the song goes, an elderly gentleman suddenly walked out from behind a stationary bus. I had no chance to avoid him, and laying him out on the floor, I was myself sent over the top, my precious cycle sliding away down the slope. Picking myself together, collecting my bike and assessing the damage, it was obvious that the bike could not be ridden further that night. As for the victim, after a short time he got to his feet and went on his way. I left for the five-mile walk back home.

My brother and I had a secret motorbike, a BSA 250. Father did not want us to have a motorbike. Brother and I frequently had to make the journey to St Mabyn from Fentrigan by horse or pushbike. As older teenagers we thought a motor bike was the ideal solution to our transport problem. We had saved up for this bike from working at Stone Farm. We rode it back to Fentrigan farm and put the bike in hiding in the bushes up in one of the fields. We were some excited with this bike but no one knew about it, especially father. Dawe came to work one morning and spoke to our father 'Maister' he said, then looking at brother and me he laughed and continued: 'There's a bit of scrap iron up in the fields, lying beside the hedge.' So the secret was out and we didn't think much of Dawe at the time for making a nuisance of himself. Anyhow father smiled and although at first concerned he got used to the idea.

It wasn't long until the BSA wasn't fast enough. Then we had a Triumph Tiger 90, and we pushed that damn thing further than we rode it. We didn't keep that one long. After the Tiger 90 I think we had a Wright. That was a hot bike. I had an accident with this one on the bend from St Tudy, taking the corner too fast, slipping on the gravel on the outside of the corner and into the hedge we went. I wasn't hurt, but lucky and even luckier that father didn't find out. Richard and I shared the bike and he often rode pillion. One day riding the bike to Stone Farm we stopped and picked up an evacuee boy who we knew and now there were three of us on this bike. We made careful and slow progress and just past Davidstow Moor on the main road, the Wadebridge to Bude Road at a bend called Woodend, the front forks cracked. I lost control of the bike and went right across the main road, on to the grass on the other side and we crumpled up into a heap, the three of us.

I don't remember the reason but I do remember on one occasion going nearly to Reading and back the same day. With no telescopic forks the long journey left me with a very sore and aching chest.

I remember going to my local pub with my BSA motor bike and after a quantity of beer deciding to go to the village hall to a dance. Some time and more drink later and fully in control, I decided to attempt the ride home. Trying to kick-start the bike I fell over with the bike on top of me. The local policeman saw this and came to my assistance, holding the bike while I made a second attempt to get going. Having started the engine and put the bike in gear, I let the clutch out too fast and sped away, losing my cap. I stopped to collect my cap that the kind policeman picked up and placed firmly on my head and I went on my way. I don't think a young man would be treated by the law in the same way nowadays.

George (Kruger) Smith and his wife Elsie worked on the farm for very many years. They had two sons and a daughter. Tom, the younger son, attended the same school as myself. He joined the navy at nineteen and was a stoker on HMS Gypsy. The Gypsy hit a magnetic mine in the North Sea in the early days of the war in 1939 with the loss of all the crew. The elder son, George, and his sister were a non-adventurous pair and did not move away from the district. The house they lived in was very spartan with just one bedroom and a kitchen with an open fireplace. Water had to be fetched from a spring, there was an outside toilet and often during a rainstorm the noise of the rain on the galvanised tin roof would be very alarming, in spite of the plywood seal. 'Kruger' as was his nickname, was dark, with a heavy moustache, looking of Spanish ancestry and spoke with a broad Cornish accent.

At the rear of the dwelling there was a small lean to shed where he kept his pig which would be eventually slaughtered for the table. Whenever anyone called to see him he made the point that you were expected to see his pig, otherwise he could become quite annoyed. 'Come here and have a look at my pig,' he would say, telling me its history and how he acquired the animal, how his wife boiled the potatoes and the feed rations, in great detail. He liked to be given praise for such remarkable achievements. 'What a lovely animal, however did you do such a fantastic job,' says I. Shaking his head, he says: 'I knows what I be doing, don't I? You don't know how to get a pig in thiccy condition.' says George. 'No, I couldn't, you have got that something special, George,' says I, to encourage him on. Another shake of the head. 'How heavy ?' 'Oh, dunno, he's a real beauty, would say twenty score, what do you think?' says I. A few grunts from the pig. Another shake of the head from the owner, becoming quite excited over his pride and joy, saying, 'Nobody can do a pig like me, can 'ee? He's a real beaut, you've got to do a vitty job, be jiggered, I'm the only man round yer that can do one like that,' says he with another shake of the head.

I HAD problems with foxes eating poultry and lambs and I decided to call in the local expert. He by night would go into the fields and make a call, very similar to the fox's nocturnal call. They would be attracted by this and come within shooting distance. A powerful torch and a loaded double-barrelled gun would finish them off. The pelts were the form of payment for this pest control service. On one occasion during daylight a fox was in close proximity to me, but wandering off. I made the whistle call, it stopped, looked around; ears pricked, and came very cautiously towards me. It stopped at a very short distance, about twenty yards distant, and slowly decided to move on and away.

I remember one day I was out walking on the farm when I came across a fox with it's leg caught in a gin trap (used for trapping rabbits), he had broken loose with the snare still attached and the fox was trying to run from me. He tried to jump over a hedge and not being successful it got caught up in the long grass and brambles. I found a stout stick with which to put poor renard out of his misery. The fox was cornered and from it's position high up in the hedge fox turned towards me and showed the white sparkling and snarling teeth before the stick came crashing down and finished him off

FOR SALMON poaching the river Camel at Helland Bridge used to be our favourite spot. I would go with my good friend and neighbour Bert Cox in his little Austin 7. We would drive to a farm near the river and use this as our base. Bert was a real character and we had some good times together. He was a good salmon poacher. Our equipment was simple and effective, a torch, a spear and a bag. I remember on this particular night we went out with our bright torch, a car headlight with a battery strapped to it. Rather heavy but very effective. On shining the torch in the river one would sometimes see as many as six to eight salmon in one pool. The salmon would usually scatter throughout the pool on being disturbed with the light. For some reason Bert couldn't do the spearing that night, he had hurt his arm I believe. I hadn't had too much experience in using the spear in the difficult conditions wearing high rubber waders in a fast flowing river on a deep uneven and slippery riverbed. Seeing by torchlight this large salmon I decided to try my luck. The river was deep and fast flowing in this part; I stood on a large stone, approximately one to two feet above the riverbed. The salmon was immediately below. Spear in hand and at the ready, Bert on the bank with the torch shining directly on the prize, I was now about to strike. Unfortunately I overbalanced and fell into the river, underestimating the depth of the salmon. I felt the salmon move away, the spear now lying on the riverbed. To retrieve the spear I was obliged to duck under the fast-flowing river not once but several times. Eventually the spear was retrieved and I, being soaked, decided to call it a night. On returning back home to Stone Farm, it being such a very cold freezing night, my frozen trousers stood upright of their own accord when I took them off in front of the fire.

There were other occasions when we were much more fortunate. We were lucky that we didn't get too many problems from the bailiffs. They existed but they were not so prevalent then as today. If things became a bit hot we played it careful and stayed away. Oh, we had some beautiful salmon; one particular salmon was like a U-boat, really huge. We could poach at almost any time of course. We went quite regularly when the salmon were running, once or twice a week and Bert and I had our regular customers. When I did catch some salmon I used to take them home, cut them up into chunks and take them on my push bike over to St Tudy, to a Dr Bailey. I would go to the back door and by pre arrangement he would buy the salmon.

COURTING DAYS

I had met a farmer's daughter at a dance in Blisland and I wanted to see her again. She told me she had a sister so I encouraged my friend Bill Masters from St Mabyn (who went down with the Ark Royal during the war) to go out on a Sunday night with me and see these girls. We called at the girl's farm entrance hoping to get a glimpse of them but all we got was their father, who seeing us parked up in Bill's car asked why we were there in such an isolated spot. We gave some excuse of having found some cattle on the road or something. Anyhow we got talking and he being a bit of a free talker and curious was interested in where we came from, I told him from Fentrigan near Warbstow. He talked on and on eventually telling of how he knew the Weary family from St Mabyn especially my aunt Adelaide and my uncle Herbert; saying he had known him well and recalling the many experiences that they had together as young men and telling me that my uncle had been a very popular fellow. He died in 1919 aged twenty eight as a result of war wounds. This farmer of course didn't realise that he was talking to the nephew of his old pal. Bill and I had difficulty in keeping serious, but he talked on and on of how well he knew the family. Oh yes, he knew my uncle well, talking of shooting parties. I asked him if he knew the other sister (my mum). 'Yes,' he said, 'but she got married to a fellow called Grigg in the Launceston area.' Bill and I had a good laugh afterwards but we missed seeing his daughters that evening.

During the early part of the war my brother Richard and I made our first trip to London in our 12.6 Vauxhall car. This was a proud possession, a second hand 1934 model for which father paid £115. On our way we were asked by dad to call at a farm near Salisbury to buy two Hampshire Down ram lambs, which we collected on our way back home, putting them in the rear part of the car. We had taken two large sacks with us and put the rams in them with only their heads outside the sacks. They kicked and struggled at first but eventually settled down for the remainder of the journey home. I had a friend whose father showed me of a photograph of a Welsh farmer who had put a large calf strapped into his sidecar as a means of livestock transport. We farmers had to show some enterprising spirit in times of fuel rationing and when livestock transport by other means was scarce.

It must have been early 1941, I was aged 21 and brother and I wanted to see the blitz and combine this with our trip for purchasing the rams. London was quite a shock; to see the devastation of the slum areas of the East End, mile after mile and street after street of houses huddled together having been blasted or burnt out. Coming as we did from the countryside we could not imagine the magnitude of being under such terrible conditions. At the time of our visit there were no houses fit to be lived in as they were all burnt or bombed out. On visiting the St Paul's area it was amazing how that Wren masterpiece was the only building left standing amidst the bombed-out ruins and rubble. We stayed with a Mr Harvey, a policeman in Hounslow, whose wife and two sons were evacuated to our farm at St Mabyn. We were very keen to see the London sights, visiting Westminster Abbey, Tower of London, St Paul's, Madame Tussaud's and lots of other places of interest. One evening I was on my own and took advantage of it by taking the

Richard, Me at Stonehenge 1940

car and going to the Hammersmith Palais-de-Dance. I met a young nurse there called Molly Armstrong a farmer's daughter from Westmorland. We had a lovely time together and we arranged a further meeting the following night at the local Adelaide public house in Hammersmith. We certainly hit off together, probably helped by me having a few drinks which brought out some hidden courage and latent desire which was lacking due to my not having sufficient experience of the opposite sex. For when I look back to those early days I was terribly shy.

We were in London for the week and on the second or third date we ended up in the back seat of the Vauxhall. Oh boy I was some nervous, I got to feeling her up a bit and both she and I got into quite an excited state, but I was too nervous and in too much of an excited sweaty state to know exactly what I was meant to be heading for. I can remember Molly also getting really excited, lying on the back seat in a state of undress, sweating and panting. There was plenty of desire by both parties but I was in too much of an excited and nervous state to lose my virginity that night. It was my last night in London and I took Molly back to her lodgings at Isleworth Hospital at two or three o'clock in the morning. The hospital gates were closed, and I had to lift her over the top of the spiked gates, over the gates she went, she inside and I stayed my side and kissed goodbye through the railings. That was the last time I ever saw her. Brother meanwhile was sitting in our digs, he didn't know where I was and was some concerned as to the whereabouts of his younger brother and the family car. For months and months she sent me little parcels in the post from London containing tobacco and cigarettes which we couldn't get, and kept in touch for two or three years. We were going to meet again. We hadn't had sex together yet and that was something I really wanted. Eventually we decided that we would meet somewhere, Bristol or somewhere, I would meet her and spend the weekend. But it never happened. The pressures of money, work, petrol being rationed and the passage of time saw to that. The experience I had with her was an opening, it broke the shyness. There was no easy protection in those days to stop you from getting a girl pregnant and that was something I was really frightened about.

Father was very much a family man, a churchwarden a god fearing man, he lived for his children, and in some ways, looking back on it now, I regret that we children were not a little more rebellious against our parents' strict authority. We were children, and children and even young adults did as their parents told them He had our lives marked out for us, meet certain people, marry certain people. Of course my brother and I we didn't take to his advice. My three younger sisters had the same problem with wanting to exercise their own will when it came to courting. They weren't allowed a lot of opportunity for socialising with the opposite sex. When they did get to get out they would go to local dances in village or town halls, it was good for them, they'd dress up, meet people, but of course anybody they met was never quite right in our parent's eyes. This caused an almighty bust up and eventually the two eldest, Betty and Adelaide left home partly as a consequence of this over protective attitude from both parents.

Betty went away up to the Midlands to a poultry farm, and then she joined the police force for quite a few years. For a long time we didn't know her whereabouts. Betty had been keen on Bill, a nice boy from a farming family near Liskeard. He was keen on her too and he used to cycle from Liskeard to Fentrigan to see her. I saw him some years ago and he enquired of Betty. He did eventually marry another but Betty never got over it. She never married. She spent most of her working life as a telephonist in the Eastbourne exchange until the old fashioned exchanges with mainly female operators were superseded by automatic exchanges. She then worked in the administration department of the Post Office until her retirement. She sold her house in Eastbourne and bought a new retirement flat in our local town of Launceston, now much nearer her two sisters and brother. Betty suffered ill health and doctors kept telling her to give up the chain smoking. She paid no attention to them and continued puffing like a train. Her health is steadily deteriorating and it seems that she now wants to sell her recently purchased flat and move into a retirement home by the sea at Bude.

My youngest sister, Sylvia, married a farmer next door to our farm at Tredarrup. She has two sons, both farmers who are married and Sylvia has three grandsons and a granddaughter. Her husband William John died tragically by taking his own life whilst his sons were still in their teens. He was a good man but a perfectionist, that was his downfall, he shot himself over a dispute with a neighbour called Frank Statton. Statton was out to cause trouble and he tried to prevent by legal means William John having access to his farm yard and farm by stating that he owned the rights of access over their short length of farm lane that was shared. William John became so unsettled and worried over the impending court case that he shot himself with his shotgun in an outbuilding and I and my sister found the body with the gun beside him. The court case did not materialize as my sister pursued Statton by all legal means to the bitter end. He was made to pay substantial sums of money to her for damages. He was basically a pig-headed, ignorant, illiterate man with a few acres and he just wanted to cause trouble. He had to accept he had no case in law. It was all so unnecessary and such a tragic waste.

Adelaide my eldest sister, she was keen on a man involved with a religious group called Toc H. She started working as a governess or nanny for the vicar and his family at nearby St Gennys when fifteen or sixteen and she made a very successful career as a governess. She eventually went on to be employed as a governess by some of the most noble and wealthy families in Britain. We were all very proud of her when she worked for a number of years as governess to Princes Andrew and Edward. She never married and has retired back to her roots at Stone farm. She spent the last ten years before recently retiring as a governess in Greece for a wealthy Greek shipping magnate and his family

Betty, Sylvia, Richard, Mum, Me, Adelaide (c1970)

There were times when of course we took our chances. I remember a time when Mum and Dad were out and I suppose it must have been prearranged by Betty and Adelaide that two fine handsome young airmen from Davidstow airfield cycled down to the farm to see them. These two boys knocked at the door, walked in and the two sisters were hard at it, scrubbing the kitchen beams. Mother had given them this chore to do and they had to finish the job first. It didn't take them long and they dressed up quickly and went out somewhere for the afternoon and evening. These two airmen became quite keen on my sisters and Betty used to be smuggled these love letters and she would hide them away in the rafters of the barn.

I had an accident in the farm lane one day whilst bringing a letter to Betty, I had probably arranged to collect it from the post office at Canworthy Water and I was riding at a walk with reins dropped over the side and not a care in the world when a dog jumped out from the hedge, horse took off, and I was off too with a nasty blow to the head which knocked me semi-conscious. I managed to stagger home and went indoors to mother with blood and mud all over my face. 'That bloody horse . . .' I was quite delirious and excited and mum was fretting around trying to get me to calm down and telling me to take my jacket off. That love letter still on my person was very much on my mind and in a moment of distraction I managed to smuggle it to Betty's eager anticipating hand. She hid these letters out of doors as to have hidden them indoors was too dangerous. I learned recently that about ten years ago one of these air force boys had been making inquiries of Betty and had tried to get in touch with her.

Dad had his marriage plans for me. A local farmer Mr Venning had in my dad's opinion a very eligible daughter for me. I remember being about twenty years old and going with father to a party at the Venning's. Mr Venning was very upstanding, in full regalia, fully breeched with his family all well turned out for this auspicious occasion. I went along with it but I cannot have been impressed by his daughter as to this very day the only thing I remember of the evening was the devout seriousness of both fathers in this coming together. We have an old country saying: 'You can take a horse to water but you cannot make it drink'. This young colt was not going to drink at this.

My parents loved each other very much but as in most marriages there were the inevitable difficult periods. Times were hard and they had a job of it struggling to bring up five children. I remember I was about twenty and there had been an argument between them at Fentrigan, what it was about I cannot remember but Mum walked. She just started to walk, we didn't know where but she was gone. Dad was looking really worried, poor old chap, and I got in the car and drove looking for her. I found her not too far from Otterham Station, and stopped the car, but she wouldn't get in the car, she kept walking. I stopped the car again, got out and tried to drag her into the car, someone else came along with a car and asked if everything was all right. I said everything was fine. She still didn't get into the car so I said to her: 'Mum, if you don't turn around and come back to dad you won't see me either. I'm off, I'll be gone too I'm going to join the Air Force or Navy or something'. I was a young man, I wanted to go. I wanted to see something of the world. I was pretty fed up with being home on the farm and doing nothing but work. I went on alone to the station I got on the first train to arrive and it started pulling out of the station. I saw my mum on the platform. She didn't get on the same train because I believe she was waiting for the Wadebridge train, I think she wanted to go to her sister Adelaide at St Mabyn. So there I was without any luggage or plans only a feeling of wanting to escape and the train was slowly pulling out of the station.

I hadn't said any goodbyes. I thought about my dear old dad back there on the farm on his own, struggling to keep it going whilst Richard was down at St Mabyn. I got off that train, a decision that lasted and was sometimes regretted. Who knows what I might have made of my life if I had stayed on that train. Of course I dealt with mum, I got her into the car eventually, took her back home and that was it, nothing was ever said by my father or mother.

My Mum (c1965)

My Mum (Hetty) at Eastbourne

I clearly remember another of my trials and tribulations of my early courting days. I wanted to go to a dance at Launceston one night and father refused to let me have the car. I had arranged to meet a girl and so I took the car anyhow, against my father's wishes. I had the most terrible evening. I never enjoyed myself, not one little tiny bit. It was going against my father's will, but I was seventeen and breaking the ice. I came home late, parked the car and went to bed. The following morning nothing was said and never a word from him on the matter.

Someone had to break the ice with my parents. My sisters couldn't do it; they were too young, so it was up to Richard my elder by four years and I to do so. The car certainly helped. The motor car is much taken for granted nowadays but for us it was the great liberator. I have lived through the twentieth century seeing the advent of more technology than I believe any other generation in history has ever been witness to. The motor car, air travel, television and radio, mechanisation of farming, the list is long and people of my generation have lived through these changes and we knew a world before now a lost world except in memory.

The motor car gave us the means of breaking out from our rural confines and conformity. In my parents' generation courting distances were governed by how far a horse and trap would carry you to your sweetheart but the motor car led to increased social mobility and mixing. Such change was difficult for my father to adjust to; he was about 45 when we got our first motor car. He wasn't keen on the idea but we persuaded him and mother was keen that we should get a car. So our very first car was something very special so special that I remember every detail.

We paid £115 for a 1934 Vauxhall 12-6 from Matthews Garage, Tavistock. Petrol was one shilling and fivepence per gallon (7p), 'Power' being the favoured brand of petrol for our car. I passed the driving test without too much difficulty aged 16 or 17. Dad did attempt to learn to drive but he could not settle with a vehicle, which did not respond to his command, as with horses, so he gave up. One Sunday on nearing the farm entrance he said he would like to try to drive the rest of the way home, I remember it distinctly, he got in, grabbed the steering wheel, started up the engine, away we went nice and steady to begin with until we came to a slight hill when the car naturally speeded up, dear old dad, he was so used to horses: 'Whoa, Whoa, Whoa,' he was saying and of course nothing happened. We weren't going very fast, I pulled on the handbrake, the car stopped safely and he never touched a car after that.

Before the car our only transport was horseback, pushbike or motorbike. The car came along for us at just the right time. Brother and I had the good fortune at a young age, I was sixteen, to take over the farming from my elderly and frail aunt at Stone Farm. She couldn't carry on so brother, myself and mum, in partnership, took the farm over and worked it. In the first two years Richard and I saved and banked £64 each. This was quite an achievement. We made some improvements and then we started doing potatoes and broccoli and then we really started to earn a lot, it was lucrative but we worked damned hard, all night sometimes, with just a few hours sleep.

If we went to a dance we would come back afterwards and go to work, trimming the broccoli, heads and tails. There would often be a train to load in the morning and we would have to get to St Kew Station with our cartloads of produce for sending to Covent Garden or Birmingham. It was great being at Stone Farm, Richard and I were there on our own, going home occasionally to Fentrigan. We could be away from the confines of home, we could socialise and mix, we could meet more people, St Maybn is not so isolated and this richer environment enriched us not only in our pockets. Meeting people, going to dances, it was all an education to us. I loved being at Stone Farm and with hindsight my brother later on made the better decision (or at least his wife made it for him) that he would continue to farm at St Mabyn and I would continue at Fentrigan

One evening I wanted to get from St Mabyn to a dance at Launceston and to meet Jean the vicar's daughter from Jacobstowe a little village near Fentrigan. Quite a round trip for one evening, but it was to be worth it for Jean was a lovely girl. I would have to have a word with my friend Bert Cox as I didn't have any transport. Bert had an Austin 7 with a canvas-topped roof full of holes. He agreed and off we went to the dance via Jacobstowe rectory to collect my Jean. She was not allowed by her parents to go out very much but I was in favour because my father had been involved with the local church. Jean was quite a sporty girl, full of fun and we had a lovely time at the dance. I remember stretching out on the seat of a chair at the dance and ripping the seat of my trousers on a furniture tack. It was about three or four inches long and we were both rather embarrassed at my mishap. Somehow we patched it up with a borrowed safety pin and we had a very pleasant evening together. It was a long night for Bert and I, going back to Jacobstowe Rectory and then in his Austin 7 with the leaking roof a further drive of twenty miles, to St Mabyn.

As for Jean she later joined the Air Force and I was very sorry to hear that, I think part of the reason she went was because of me, I had been rather foolish with moves that I made towards another girl and Jean was somewhat understandably offended. She did eventually get her own back on me, no doubt about that, as I was very fond of her. Our dissolution I rather took to heart in no small way. Later we did write occasionally. I wasn't too happy with this, I was a little bit jealous of her having joined up and I was still at home on the farm. We weren't allowed to join up, classified as essential civilian workers for the war effort. I don't think the war had actually started but there was certainly a lot of talk of war and a state of being on a war footing.

Jean eventually married and went to live at Dobwalls. Jean had a brother called Edmund and he taught me to drive a car. He later went to Jamaica for several years as a vicar and when he retired he came back to live in Fowey. I went to his funeral quite recently and I saw Jean who was delighted to see me. I went into Derriford hospital last year with some heart problems and there was another patient in my ward at Derriford who was from Dobwalls who knew Jean and her husband very well. He passed the message onto Jean that I was ill in hospital and she came to see me. I was quite overwhelmed and very pleased to see her.

The car salesman at Matthew's Garage, Tavistock where we had recently bought our first car was a fellow called Dennis Bruford. Now Dennis had a stepsister Joan, whose mother Alice in her first marriage was married to my Uncle Herbert. She had had twins by him but they died very young and after Uncle's death at the age of 28 she later married a Mr Greenslade who died of a heart attack whilst watching Plymouth Argyle. Joan was her daughter by Greenslade and she later married Mr Bruford a teacher at Kelly College. I remember some malicious family gossip that Alice had allegedly over the years kept in touch with my aunt who farmed at Stone hoping that one day she might receive something from her ex sister-in-law. There was no settlement for Alice and their relationship was soured over this matter. It could not have been that bad as shortly after buying the car I was invited by Mr and Mrs Bruford to stay with them at Tavistock for a few days.

It was Joan who took me to my very first dance. I remember being very shy for I had not had the opportunities given to other children fortunate enough to be living in the towns of making friends and developing social skills. I was a slow beginner but I came to love going to dances. I became quite a good ballroom dancer. Tavistock Town Hall was my first venue. I was quite young, sixteen or seventeen and I had never been alone with a girl, very shy I was, and it was Joan who escorted me out in what I suppose you could term my 'coming out'

Amongst all these girls I began to colour up, this one and that one would ask me for a dance and I would just freeze and blush. Eventually I did decide to give it a try after all I had been so looking forward to going out and dressing up in my smart suit and so I went dancing. One problem, I couldn't dance, I had no idea how to do any of the movements, the girls were very patient and they taught me and helped me through an embarrassing time. As the night wore on I enjoyed myself. The music was dance band music, the Glen Miller type.

After that I became a dance fanatic and I used to go to Bodmin to dance classes once a week. I did try a bit of tap dancing but ballroom dancing was my favourite. I didn't know many girls but the few I did know had to put up with my rather clumsy beginner's style but I gradually became quite a good dancer. I mastered quite a few, the waltz, the valeta, and the foxtrot. It was also an excellent strategy for meeting girls and I did enjoy dancing. I kept the touch; I was frequently complimented even in my seventies by dancing partners at hunt balls or dances of how stylish and confident I was. The man needs to be confident in the role of leader in the dance. The man must lead and the lady must follow, but she can only do so if her partner knows the movements.

My friend and neighbour at St Mabyn, Ken Simcock, and I frequently used to go to dances at Wadebridge Town Hall. Ken was a great pal of mine in those days. He lives in St Austell now and I clearly remember him and I chatting animatedly away in front of the hearth fire at Stone discussing how this new invention in America called the combine harvester was going to do away with work. He too was a farmer's son and anything to reduce the daily toil was bound to be a blessing to us. He only had a pushbike and I had a motor bike and sometimes on the way back from a Wadebridge dance he would be riding pillion passenger with his pushbike sort of straddling his shoulders. I got him home anyway and we had some great times together.

While at St Maybn brother and I spent some time with various friends and girls, but I never really got myself involved with anyone until I met Phyllis Davey. She was my first love. I was nineteen she was six years my senior and married. I was infatuated with Phyllis, the attractive wife of a local farmer. We had met at the local village dances and had written letters and after a few months we became very close. I had not at that time had any sexual experience and I was very shy. We met and had a near sexual experience, to me anyway, at Bodmin Beacon, in a hayfield. This was a beginning of hope for the ultimate. We arranged a further meeting. I was to call at her farmhouse one evening when her husband was off doing his Home Guard duties for the night, the plan was that I would stay the night.

I was very excited at the prospects and set off on my pushbike. Calling at the house, I knocked at the door and a window from the bedroom opened and a man's voice called: 'Who's there?' I was standing at the front porch, not knowing what to do; I began to sweat and stood hidden from him. It was a beautiful moonlight night. I heard the window close. I ran to a hedge and flattened myself up against it but unfortunately fell backwards into a bed of stinging nettles. A window immediately above me opened and he again called: 'Who's there?' I froze, being possibly visible to the full view of him in the moonlight. The window closed. I lay still for a short while then I ran as fast as I could and going down across a hilly field, I fell but kept moving by rolling. I had to make a detour back to find my cycle and I returned home. I felt lucky at not being caught but very disappointed as that night was going to be my first full sexual experience. I never did have sex with her.

Richard and I one night were supposed to go to Stone Farm with the car. The Royal Cornwall show in those days was held in various places in Cornwall, and that particular year it was held at Bude, Instead of going to Stone Farm we took the car and went to Bude to the big annual show dance. This was without our parents knowing, they weren't too keen on us attending dances. I met a girl from down near St Ives, a farmer's daughter who was showing some cattle at the show. I palled up with this girl, it was wonderful, I really enjoyed the evening and that was how brother and I had to get our pleasure. We had to be a little crafty without our parents knowing too much of what was going on.

A few years later I met an ex-GI bride from Milton Abbot, I was introduced to her by a local cattle dealer and we arranged to meet at Milton Abbot and go on to a Hunt Ball at Ashburton. I left the farm early in the evening, it was winter and dark, I called at a garage just outside Launceston for petrol and again at Tavistock on the Plymouth Road I stopped to have the tyres tested for pressure. Going on to Milton Abbot and picking up my girl we called at the Halfway House for a drink and I used the spare change in my pocket to pay for the drinks.

We arrived fairly late at Ashburton with every intention of having a good exciting evening; I was dressed in my best evening suit with bow tie. She was extremely attractive and dressed in a long flowing evening gown. We were met by and I was introduced to some of her friends. I went to the bar to get the necessary drinks. I confidently ordered the drinks, put my hand in my pocket to draw out my wallet. It was not there. This made me feel terrible and I had to try to explain. However, friends of hers saw my predicament and came over to offer help. We decided to return to the nearby Halfway House pub, but to no avail. Returning to the ball, I borrowed £10 from this friend of hers and tried to relax, and after a few beers did just that.

On leaving the ball in the early hours and returning to Milton Abbot, having dropped her off to her home, I returned to my earlier stops with a faint hope of finding the lost wallet. Driving on to the garage forecourt I happened to see through the headlights a dark object. Stopping, to my surprise there was my wallet, complete, everything intact.

On another occasion I lost my wallet containing £18 one morning at Stone Farm in a pigsty. I retraced my steps to the sty and I found it all chewed up by the pigs in about six inches of pig manure. Opening the door and letting the pigs free, I decided to try and salvage the eighteen pounds if possible. The pigs had champed the paper into small pieces, I had to go through the dung with a toothcomb, bit by bit, and it was difficult to identify dung from paper. However with persistence I eventually salvaged twelve or thirteen pounds. The bank numbers had to correspond and money being very scarce and hard to get I was pleased and very lucky to salvage what I did.

THE WAR

I believe the war had already started when the authorities decided to build an aerodrome on Davidstow Moor and some farms, including Tom Heard's farm at Larkaborough, were demolished. He recently died aged nearly a hundred and he must have had quite an experience as a newly married man. He was the son of our neighbouring farmer at Hendra and on getting married in the early 1940s took a tenancy on a Duchy farm at Larkaborough. He wasn't there long before the airforce requisitioned the whole of Davidstow moor and bulldozed flat his farm. Other farms and the Camelford to Altarnun road were also demolished. The airfield was never fully utilised as it proved to be generally fogbound, except during one night when scores of Flying Fortresses were directed to Davidstow as the only fog-free airfield in South West England. With only a small amount of fuel left after a bombing raid on Germany, it was recognised that the airfield was paid for in that one night. After the war it was never used again, it fell into disrepair, the control tower in ruins. The concrete runways are still there and used by nothing more than a local power-gliding club and the moorland sheep and cattle for basking in the summer sun. My memories are of the American flyers, their exciting ways, their visits to local dances, their lively music and that night when Davidstow by providence saved the day for our boys returning from Germany.

Another wartime memory of the airfield is that of the local rabbit trapper named Stan Creeper. He continued his unhindered lifestyle laying his traps and collecting his rabbits near or on the newly constructed security conscious aerodrome. Collecting his trapped rabbits by night with the use of a torch, he was apprehended by air force security, taken in and questioned at length, them thinking he was a German spy. Stan was a local character, wiry, short and with a streak of violence when aroused. He did not take kindly to the authorities disrupting his trapping. However the locals missed him after a few days, inquiries were made and he was eventually freed after his identity was established.

Ziebelt Otten or Zip as we called him was a prisoner of war who was billeted with us at Fentrigan during the war before my marriage and he stayed for a time after the war and after my marriage working and lodging with us. I liked and respected Zip, he was educated, spoke good English and he hadn't wanted to be part of the Third Reich.

He was a farmer's son who knew all about farming, he had a good understanding of English, which made life easier for the family. He was large, sturdy, balding, and wore thick lens spectacles, very pleasant and quite jovial. He mixed in with our family and was treated well. He was also good company. I recall he would, after his day's work, join my mum in the kitchen. Zip and her had a very good rapport and they would sit in the chimney corner beside the open fire with the kettle singing and enjoy a cup of tea together. He loved his tea and so did mother; and they would sit there talking of his family back home.

After the war Zip stayed with us for two to three years and after he was repatriated he married a German war widow. Over the many years since those far-off times he and I kept in touch by correspondence almost every Christmas. He knew all about the difficulties of my first marriage to Marjorie Bayly, he was with me at the time and he knew that the marriage was on the rocks. He didn't tell me until it was all over that he had little confidence in that marriage ever surviving

I regret not having made the effort of a reunion with him, I liked him so very much and I was most saddened to receive a letter from his wife a few years ago telling me that Zip had died. He too had his sad loss of a loved one during the war; his only brother disappeared somewhere on the Russian Front.

I recall a few episodes whilst he was with us. Trying one day to blow up some rocks with gunpowder, he realised that after lighting the fuse, the gunpowder didn't go off. It had been stored by my father a few years previously, and had become damp. Being either brave or foolish, he laid it on a flat tray to dry near the open fireplace, at first keeping it away at a safe distance. Getting bolder with time going on, he decided to edge the powder a little closer to the fire, it eventually became warmer but, not being confined, made one terrific swish and a slight bang. The whole kitchen was immediately enveloped in black smoke, which took a long time to clear away. We both edged our way through the smoke to the back door. Zip was singed around the eyebrows and hair plus a slight burn on the face. I, being at a distance, did not get any burns. After the smoke had dispersed and on returning to the kitchen hearth area, we still smelt burning. Looking up to the ceiling, the blast and heat from the explosion had caught alight the beams above.

We were cleaning out the cattle houses, taking dung from the farmyard to a distant field to put into heaps, later to spread with prongs, while Zip went to and from the field with the horses and cart. When he had been missing for a considerable time I became concerned and went to look for him. I found that the cart had upset, the horses unhinged and Zip was upside down with blood, mud and scratches on his body. He told me that he was sitting on the front of the cart, the front horse turned too quickly on getting to the farm drive from the gate and the back horse had no choice except to follow the turn of the leading horse. The wheels went into the hedge and finally the cart went over with Zip trapped inside. It was a very dangerous position because if the horses had not stopped he would have been dragged along in the boxed area of the cart. However, to get out of this he had to bodily lift the cart somehow with his shoulders in a cramped position, high enough to get out the tailboard lynch pin, when he could then creep out. How he managed to do this I cannot imagine.

At the same time as we had Zip we were sent another POW to help out at busy times, a tall, blonde, blue-eyed Nazi of Prussian blood, one of Hitler's 'Aryan' super breed. He was not with us long, not any use at all for farm work. Zip and he did not get along, they hated each other, and he had so little experience of how to handle farm tools that we were pleased when he was taken away. He had hurt his shoulder and he was apparently taken to a hospital for treatment. He had probably intended all along to do as little as possible and to cause as much inconvenience to the authorities as possible.

Me and Italian POW (Micheal) 1943

Michael was the first Italian POW we had and he stayed on the farm for a while. He was a nice lad, from Southern Italy, I think his parents had a post office or shop there. He wasn't much use to us but he pitched in anyway and did what he could. Eventually he went back to the camp and he returned to Italy some time after the war.

At St Mabyn we grew approximately ten acres of early potatoes. Italian prisoners were camped nearby so we employed approximately twenty men brought daily on a lorry guarded by their transport driver who brought them to the farm. He carried a rifle and was responsible for their well being, but they were never any trouble. These Italians were not very good workers and we had a certain amount of difficulty in getting them organised. They were a cunning lot and would use every trick to make things difficult. They were put in pairs, each at a given distance, marked out so that when that area was picked they could rest until we came around with the potato lifting machine pulled by horses. At times they would try to hold up the work by complaining that someone had moved their marker to their disadvantage.

We also employed Land Army girls, some were very good. I well remember this girl who, when working in the field with potatoes or broccoli, which my brother and I grew, she kept cleaning out the dirt from under her very long fingernails and this was, I thought, quite funny she needed her nails clipping. My mate Ken Simcock, a local farmer's son decided enough was enough and caught this Land Army girl with the flashy nails. We took some scissors, held the girl and cut off the long claws. She screamed, kicked, argued, but however in the end we succeeded. She was from Workington in Cheshire, tall with a good figure, a truly lovely person who took it all in good spirit, her townie ways being broken by the local farmer's sons. Quite a few of these girls were attractive and very forward because they came from towns, but we boys were country yokels and we weren't lively enough for them. On one occasion I met a land girl at a St Maybn village hall at a Young Farmers dance. She wanted me to take her home after the dance but to take her to the nearby farm where she worked and was billeted she would have to sit upon the handlebars of my push-bike. I sat her on the handlebars, legs out, she leaning back against me and I started pedalling about a mile to where she lived. When I got to the farm entrance I could not stop and we crashed in a heap together with a few minor scratches and bruises but we did have a good laugh.

Another Land Army girl called Phyllis Baldwin came from Brixton, London and she was billeted on a neighbour's farm belonging to Commander Blewett. His wife an ex-Wren was looking after their small farm whilst he was away in the war. Phyllis spent her time generally helping out on the farm and looking after the farm animals
The Blewetts neighbour Jack Symons had only been married to Muriel a few days and on his return from honeymoon Ken Simcock, Phyllis and myself decided to play a practical joke on him. It was a very windy and wild night, putting and wrapping bags around our boots to deaden any noise, we proceeded to tie the doors of his old cottage, whitewash the windows, climb onto the roof and block the chimney. We also unhinged his front garden gate and left it standing and leaning against the post looking as if it was still hung. In paint on the old shed door, we wrote: 'Jack and Muriel went up the hill to fetch a pail of water. Jack came down with half a crown but not for fetching water.'
Leaving unheard we waited to hear the results of our prank and welcome home present. Jack was a big boaster, liar and a general nuisance. Phyllis, living next door, eventually told us that in the morning, finding the doors and windows blocked and darkened and being smoked out because of the chimney blockage, he had difficulty in getting out of the house, and when he eventually got himself disentangled and made for the gate, in his hurry he pushed it and fell over on the gate. It was not possible for a long time to remove our ditty on the shed door; it caused a good laugh with us and others in the village for a long time.

THE WAR Ministry told us what we had to grow on the farm. Laws were brought in giving authority to the War Agricultural Committee who used to come around to see the farms and tell us which fields we should plough and which crops to plant. This field goes into wheat, that one into oats and that field into something else like potatoes. This was the best thing that had ever happened to Fentrigan because we had to plough the fields. The old pasture was tough, dry, lifeless, by putting in the plough in it made the land a lot more productive. We had to renew the pastures with better grasses, new grasses, to produce more hay, which in turn allowed other fields to be turned over to growing cereals. We were given subsidies to go and get sand and to add livestock manure to the fields. Fields were small and all the work was done by horses, we didn't have a tractor and all this war effort was a considerable amount of extra work. Normally we didn't plough more than about ten acres a year, and that was limited to certain fields which were farmed on a regular rotation of grass, oats, turnips and grass. The local agricultural committee consisted mainly of retired farmers, coming around to your farm dictating what must be done. Some farmers didn't like it, some did. The committee was basically interested in ploughing up the soil, renewing the pastures. More hay and cereals was what they wanted.

During the war food was rationed, and a special permit was required through the Ministry of Food to slaughter a pig or lamb for one's own consumption. A pig was killed annually on the farm for the family consumption, and cured in the trundle. This was a long-standing tradition – the pig killing. As youngsters we used the pig's bladder for a football. Our sport didn't last that long but we got some pleasure from it. The pig would be killed in one of the cattle sheds, a rope tied tightly around the upper part of the mouth, strung up to a beam and the throat then cut, making sure to cut the main jugular vein. On one occasion father's knife slipped, the rope came away from the pig's mouth and it went charging through the door with blood flying everywhere. Eventually it collapsed and died in the farmyard, where we had to do the necessary cleaning, getting the bristles off by using scalding hot water and a special scraper. The pig would then be butchered and hams prepared for smoking and the rest of the carcass preserved in brine. In the dairy was a granite trundle with a wooden cover. It took a lot of rock salt and my job was to cut up the pig. The brine had to be changed and the hams, shoulder, bacon etc turned over, and the process repeated. When cured the hams were put into muslin bags and hung in the larder. Nothing was wasted; the intestines were cleaned and used for sausage skins. The trotters and head were used for brawn; the bacon was very fat and was a base for the breakfast egg and potatoes.

I recollect another tale about pigs and permits. This story about a pig in a pub and the Ministry was told to me by a retired policeman who I knew well sometime after the war. A local pub had a few acres and no killing permit, but word got around that a pig or two were slaughtered and stored in the pub. The Ministry of Food got wind of this and arrived at the pub with the local constable to give the premises a thorough search, taking the owner by surprise. However the constable being a local stood over the well in the kitchen area that was covered by a carpet, whilst the search was carried out by the men from the Ministry. The constable's role was supposedly to keep his watchful eye on the landlord during the search. Of course they found nothing and departed empty handed. The illegal store of pig meat hanging in the cool well was eventually shared out.

Living in a remote area, eight miles from the nearest town of Camelford, we didn't receive newspapers. We did hear the war bulletins on the radio but my father was not keen on it. Brother and I did have a radio at Stone Farm and I remember the Ecko radio and the battery becoming discharged every week when we were absent at Fentrigan. Our parents didn't talk about the war very much to us, perhaps it was because we were young men and they were frightened of us joining up or because of wanting to protect us. Brother and I followed events partly through the radio but also through talking with other young farmers on those relatively rare occasions when we could lift our heads from the grindstone.

Farmers sons had special status as a reserved occupation, I certainly didn't consider myself special, I would rather have joined up I was nineteen at the outbreak of war and I wanted to join the RAF. But my duty was to continue farming, looking after the land. Dig for Victory was the slogan. We farmers had to grow the food to feed the country, and so we weren't called up.

It was during the war years that I used to spend Christmas's with my aunt at Stone Farm to help her with the farming. She at that time was in good health and we used to go out and accumulate a lot of wood, which was stored over the summer period and bring it into the very large kitchen, which had a huge open fire. In the evening, we would work with the crosscut saw cutting short logs for the fire.

FIRST MARRIAGE

MY FIRST marriage was to the girl next door. The only daughter of the neighbouring farmer. Fate dictated that we should marry. I now write this fifty years later and with the benefit of hindsight but if I was to live my life over again then I am sure that this ill-starred marriage would still have occurred. What were the circumstances that led me, drove me, so inexorably to marry Marjorie Bayly.

The courting happened during the war years. Petrol was rationed and with travel restrictions and a heavy farm work programme, there was little time or energy left over for enjoyment. There was the rural isolation, the restricting influence of my parents, the limited opportunities for meeting the opposite sex, the fact that there were so few girls. There was also probably the subliminal influence of my parents with their own unspoken blessing for my courting of the neighbouring farmer's daughter. Their horizons never went far beyond the farm gate. My horizons were raised to different and further aspirations. Circumstances dictated that for me it was 'Work, work and yet more work'. It was expected of me and my brother that we would leave school at the earliest opportunity and work on the farm. That was the way it was with our family in those days. How so very different from modern times with the youth of today having so many opportunities. I know that as a father I always encouraged my children to go out into the world and find themselves, to play sports to do all the normal things that their contemporaries do and take for granted. Such vision and opportunities were denied to me in my teenage years and early twenties. There was no rebellion, not to any significant amount from me, you obeyed your parents and you did as you were told. That was my upbringing.

Marjorie was about twenty-three years old when we started seeing each other on a regular basis. I had known of her of course for some years as she was the neighbouring farmer's daughter and she had an elder brother called Edward. They farmed at Trevilian in the valley opposite.

Marjorie was serious by nature with a limited sense of humour. She had natural auburn curly hair and was rather short in height with a rosy complexion. She was a volunteer for the local nursing group and I was in the Home Guard. We had to attend meetings which entailed training and some travel to various places for rifle range shooting and day and night exercises. This brought us together to a limited degree. Around that time I was invited to be the best man to another neighbouring farmer who married Marjorie's aunt. This was the beginning of the development of a closer relationship with Marjorie

I went out with her for two to three years before we eventually married in 1946. There were times I wanted to get out of the courtship but I took the plunge and hoped to leave my previous shyness and courting difficulties behind me. I wanted to try and put the past behind me and build a future in our new home at Fentrigan. My father actually wanted my elder brother Dick to take over the farm from him on his marriage two years earlier. Dick had married a local farmer's daughter Mary Parsons from Trerose Farm at Otterham but they made a decision together that they didn't want to stay and farm at Fentrigan. So instead they initially went to Stone Farm, St Mabyn where brother and I were partners.

When I subsequently married the partnership at Stone was dissolved and I continued to live at Fentrigan with my new wife. Dick and Mary still continued to farm at St Mabyn but also took on a large farm tenancy at Porthmissen near Padstow.

My Brother Richard's Wedding (1944)

My first Wedding (Mum, Adelaide, Sylvia, Richard, Me, Betty, Dad) (1946)

My father, mother and sisters went to live at Stone Farm which had been owned by mother's side of the family, the Weary's. My Aunt Adelaide had bought the farm for £11,500 from her landlord Mrs Gatley of Liskeard and when my aunt died in 1938, she being childless left it to my mum. Mum and Dad lived there in semi-retirement until my dad died in 1955. My brother and his wife Mary continued to farm at Stone but went to live at Porthmissen Farm near Padstow and continued living and farming there until my brother's death in 1990. His widow Mary still lives there and their son Brian and his two sons Neil and Mark Grigg continue to farm there and also at Stone farm to this day.

We got married at the local Methodist chapel, the Grigg's were church, it was the bride's family who were chapel folk. We returned to the bride's farmhouse for the reception, and later went to Launceston railway station for the start of our honeymoon in Llandudno, North Wales. The war had just finished, troops were still prominent everywhere. I remember at Launceston station seeing a friend from a family I knew quite well saying goodbye to his wife on the platform, I recall the contrast, the sadness of how he was leaving his loved one and how we were starting a new life together.

Arriving at our destination, we stayed in a guest house in a part of the town overlooking the sea and the Great Orme, it was a pleasant atmosphere and the family made us welcome. We had various trips to beauty spots around and I was quite happy, but I had a strange feeling about Marjorie, that something was not quite as it should be. She would isolate herself from any outside conversation and did not appear to want to enter into any adventure. This was also noted in her attitude towards my sexual advances. I recall how the conversation would drift towards her mum and dad, which I fully understood and accepted, she being an only daughter and not having a very good relationship with her brother.

On Honeymoon at Llandudno Pier

Honeymoon 1946   *Honeymoon 1946*

Having returned from our one-week honeymoon we began to build our future together. At first the marriage appeared to be normal but a few incidents occurred that I was not too happy with. I remember my dad called at the farm on a wet and windy day. Normally he would have been invited in if only for a cup of tea. He was not made welcome. Both my parents stayed away from the farm, my wife being of a jealous nature. My parents and family declined any contact rather than cause a rift. This caused me to speak up and I found out later that any and everything done was referred back to her mum and dad. Her father was very selfish and his views were always correct and had to be respected. He would go to any extreme to crush any opposition.

My farming was my own and Marjorie's affair. The business was in my name and my desire was to improve my lot by getting together a dairy herd and moving forward. The basic horse machinery was gradually changed to modern tractor equipment. My dad had given me £500, some livestock and oddments. That was quite a lot of money in those days. The terrible winter of 1946-47, our first year together, depleted our sheep flock from fifty to twenty five ewes and the diseases of enterotoxaemia and haemorrhagic septicaemia resulted in even more deaths. We were isolated for six weeks in the snow and could not get out from the farm. I did not have a car; my only form of transport was a motorcycle.

Such terrible weather during our first year of farming brought many difficulties so we had a daily help for my wife. As time progressed she wanted to improve the house and have a few modern conveniences. We had an Aga cooker installed and generally brought the farmhouse up to a more modern standard. Of course there was no electricity or running water. Water was pumped up by an old lead hand pump from a well in the back part of the house. Improvements were required and I set to, working hard to make improvements both to the farm and farmhouse. Mr Bayly, my father-in-law, began to give his views on my new farming enterprises. I did not argue with him, but I wanted to go my own way. This state of affairs went on for some time.

I had by this time a feeling Marjorie was being strongly influenced by her parents and things became quite worrying. Zip told me he thought her father and mother were out to cause trouble and no good would come of it. I had redecorated the house and bought some expensive wallpaper for a lounge, Marjorie decided to tear it off the wall because of one or two pieces were not joined properly. This annoyed me but she would not follow discussion through so that a compromise could be reached, but would go quiet and take the story to her parents. This caused more friction and she, now being pregnant, did not improve. With her parents exerting a powerful influence on her, she thought that it would be possible to stay at her parents' house. This was not readily acceptable by me but at first I went along with it. This went on for a while, staying with me, then going to stay with them in their cottage approximately one and a half miles from the farm. Bayly had retired now and his son was farming his enterprise. His retirement did not improve his dealings with me, he did not approve of his son-in-law, and there was nothing I could do to alter that fact. When Marjorie came to me and slept, on one occasion during the night I was suddenly awakened by shouting outside the window: 'Marjorie dear, don't stay there, come home.' She replied: 'I will be home tomorrow, dad.'

One evening I went with Zip on my motorcycle to Bude fair, he encouraged me to have a go at having my fortune told. At first I laughed at the idea but after persuasion I entered the caravan, paid and showed my palm. The gypsy woman looked into the glass and started to talk. As time wore on and she explained to me my past, my character and future, I became thoughtful and after the reading I asked her the meaning of her statement: 'Beware! Beware! There is someone who is very close to you acting like a snake in the grass.' I thought of who this might be, but I kept it close to my chest. On looking back her prophecies were without doubt close to how events unfolded. Incidentally I have never been to a fortuneteller since.

It was also about this time that I had a dream. A dream so clear, a vision, a strong premonition I was in a court with the judge in the high chair, jury, my parents, her parents, Marjorie at one end and me the other end, fighting it out. This went on for some time, then a space of ages, emptiness, never to see her again. I awoke, she was asleep beside me but I did not forget that dream. I have never forgotten it.

During our courtship and after our marriage, I gave up a lot of my pleasures because of her not enjoying them or not wanting to join in. I enjoyed dancing, an occasional drink, but she seemed totally uninterested and when on a rare occasion we did go out it usually ended in disaster. In fact to sum it up, looking back it was a mistake on my part to give up my pleasures to please her whims, but at the time I wanted our marriage to be a success.

Bayly was rarely seen in his car, his preferred mode of transport was his bicycle, which he rode frequently from his retirement farm cottage to his son's farm and at times to my home. He was usually dressed in boots, breeches and leggings. He was rather sturdy in build at about 5ft 8ins tall, silver wavy hair, a rather tight mouth and very shifty eyes. When talking to him he would use a lot of body movements, his arms would move frequently but with hardly any eye contact. He was in his mid fifties. His experience of the world outside was quite limited, he was proud of the fact that he had never been on a train, and the furthest he had been was Exeter. I had a feeling that he would be worried if he lost sight of his chimney top. My wife also disapproved of travel; even my going out on business regarding the farm was questioned.

Bayly was in the habit of rambling on about his successes, his farming, and his money. He liked to gossip about other people and seemed to enjoy talking of failures or people's downfall. He had no sense of humour whatsoever; this also applied to his wife and daughter. I did stop and listen to his ramblings, being patient and understanding, and because he was my father-in-law, but I was perhaps naive as to his motives. As time progressed he became even more aggressive to me, I was trying to compromise but losing the battle. He was strange at times, sometimes talking normally, giving useful advice and giving me some small confidence in him. Just prior to the birth of Janet, my wife was still spending time with her parents and sometimes with me at the farm. One saw the logic of her being with her parents for some of the time while she was heavily pregnant. In May of 1948 Janet was born at the farmhouse. Marjorie's mother was present at the birth; not having a telephone I had to go to a kiosk at the village to notify the doctor. I could not make contact so I had to travel to another kiosk. Having got through to the doctor, saying it was urgent, he was not available, so the village nurse was sent for. When I arrived back at the farm the baby was just born. The nurse arrived shortly afterward. Eventually I had some explaining to do as to why the terrible delay, as if I were to blame.

At that time I sincerely hoped that my wife and baby would stay with me at the farm and we would hope to have a happier relationship together. This did happen and things seemed to improve now that the baby was born. Having Janet gave me the responsibility for making a future for us all, to build a home together and have all the joys of being parents to a loved one. For a few months her parents did not frequent the farm so regularly and we settled down and got on with our lives as normal. I thought we seemed a happy, normal couple. Trouble started again around September of that year with interference by her parents. She again went to stay with them, taking baby Janet with her. She stayed with them for quite some time; while there the baby was being fed on milk produced from the farm. It was my expected duty to take milk every evening to their house for the baby. I felt tired at times, especially after working hard in the harvesting period.

I remember going to their house one evening and said I was going to visit my parents that evening at St Mabyn, about fifteen miles away on my motorcycle. Bayly at the time was not at home but Marjorie and her mother Lettie said that I was not to go but stay with my wife and baby instead. I did not agree and they locked the door so that I could not get out of the house. A few words passed between us, not too complimentary, then I slapped my wife's face, the only time I ever used any force on her. The scene that followed was quite frightening and extraordinary. Her mother screamed at me full of terrible accusations, becoming nearly breathless, down on her knees, thumping the floor with her fists, speechless with saliva drooling from her mouth. Marjorie joined in too saying that

I should do this and that to please her, not to laugh so much and be more serious towards her. I do have a sense of humour, especially when under duress at times like this, and my laughter in this situation only inflamed their wrath. I was beginning to realise that I was in the midst of madness, locked in the house, I stood by the welsh dresser in the kitchen and put my hands deeper into my pockets where they would be safer from provocation. After a long time Bayly returned. He listened to all; but nothing was resolved. He did eventually let me out of the house but it was then too late to visit my parents. I left for home on my motorbike.

After several attempts to get Marjorie and Janet back, finally in about mid-October she and our five-month old baby returned to live with me. Naturally I was very happy to have them back and I put every effort into the relationship so that I could keep them with me. Occasionally Bayly and his wife Lettie visited us, at times they were quite aggressive toward me, on one occasion Bayly twisted my arm behind my back On another occasion Mrs Bayly held her walking stick to my head, threatening me. I did tell her that if she felt any better she could hit me with it. On a further occasion I was being accused by my mother-in-law of not being a suitable father and incapable of looking after the baby. She was standing in front of the Aga and she suddenly threw the baby at me. This was done so swiftly that I was fortunate not to have missed catching Janet. It was apparent from this and other episodes that she had a vile temper, quite uncontrollable.

There were times that Bayly would come to coax my wife away from me. Sometimes during the night he would call up at the bedroom window to inquire of her well being and ask her to return. I have often in later years reflected on his actions and wondered why Bayly was so possessive of his only daughter, was there a secret kept hidden?

On 6 November 1948, a Monday morning, Bayly came to the farm and unknown to me took his daughter out for a drive. The following day I met him in the farm drive, pushing the pram out of the lane with Janet inside. He told me that Marjorie did not feel too good and she was staying for a few days with him and she wanted Janet with her. This I was obliged to accept but I was not at all happy with this recurring situation. The following morning, Wednesday, my workman Ashley Davey and the girl home help who lived with us in the farmhouse and myself were suddenly confronted with an irate Bayly, who had come together with his son and their farm workers to collect the furniture. Their tractors and trailers were in the farmyard at the ready. Ashley Davey went off to work, leaving me quite stunned to face the unknown. I asked for Marjorie: 'When is she coming back to me?' He replied: 'She is never coming back to you again and I shall see to that.' He said: 'I have come to take the furniture and other things.' I said: 'What have I done that you should do this to me?' He said: 'You have done enough and now it's my turn'. I replied, in utter confusion: ' I've done nothing wrong, I will go to my grave with a clear conscience.' His immediate reply was, coming close to me: 'Go on then, Bill, do it.' I was so stunned my heart sank and I felt suicidal for a moment or two but I said nothing more to him. I vowed never to think of it again. I just wanted to get even with him.

Walking out in confusion, not knowing what to do to stop him, I decided to go to the local policeman, Rodney Pethick. He told me that he could not interfere in a domestic dispute, but advised me to go to a solicitor.

At solicitor Roger Parnell's office at Launceston, I was presented with facts I did not wish to hear. You cannot force your wife to live with you if she does not want to, and that the mother should have the baby, especially at the tender age of six months. I said: 'They are out there taking away the furniture.' His reply was quite direct and definite, that if she wanted her furniture she was perfectly entitled to it. I recall leaving that office in tears. Returning to the farm some time after, it felt as though a plague of locusts had attacked. Everything movable in the house had gone, the stair carpets, fittings, curtains, lamps, nothing left except my violin and a lot of my clothes lying in the corner of the bedroom. I went to the bedroom, knelt down and cried bitterly amongst my clothes strewn across the floor. He could not take the house or farm away, but I had to arrange that our live-in girl home help returned to her previous employ immediately. I had no bed, so I spent the next ten days or so sleeping on the straw in an outhouse. In those post war days furniture was bought on a points system because of scarcity. We had bought some new furniture and had used up all the points allocated to us. I had to wait until a sale of furniture came up by public auction and I was able to buy in replacements from Ethy Barton near Lostwithiel. Some of the furniture was quite large, an oak sideboard, being part of a banqueting suit by Maples of London, in three pieces a large central mirror with overhang, two pillars with lion wood carvings, recess with cupboards and drawers with bronze fittings and handles. The wardrobe was also very large, in three sections. I also bought beds and other necessary things. My brother with his lorry helped to deliver my purchases to the farm where I managed to get myself together in the farmhouse after having an uncomfortable week or so in the straw.

On the day after the forced removal, I made an urgent appointment to visit a firm of solicitors at St Austell, getting an appointment with Stanley Sampson, pouring out all my problems. He wrote a letter to my wife asking her to return to the matrimonial home. On returning to the farm I was told that Bayly had been again and had taken some chickens and a fowls house. I was going around like a zombie, being shattered to the core and asking myself, 'Why? Why? Why? What have I done?'

On the Saturday he again came and demanded the geese. I refused to let him have them. I could not restrain him so I asked my workman to go to a phone and call the police. Within a short time the police arrived and tried to restrain him, but to no use. He eventually took the geese; the police of course were there only to keep the peace and not to take sides. I had already given the police full details of what had happened a couple of days previously. I soon realised I was on my own with this. I got nothing more than polite sympathy from the police and their support was rather limited. They perceived it to be a domestic dispute and kept a watchful eye on the situation. I did not attempt to touch Bayly. Probably if I had done I would have killed him, and it is possible the police had thought of that.

I hadn't wanted to involve my parents. My mum and dad were staying in Solihull at the time with their eldest daughter, Adele. They were not encouraged by me to come to the farm, as I wanted to sort things out my way without any interference from anyone. Zip my faithful POW who worked with me on the farm had gone, repatriated back to Germany some months before. All I had was a very faithful border collie dog called Ben and he was fantastic towards me, nuzzling his nose into my arms and looking at me with those wonderful searching eyes, telling me that he knew and cared. He kept very close to me, knowing somehow that I needed help and he wanted to help me. My violin was a wonderful inspiration to me. I am not a good player but so long as I was making music, the relaxation gave me a sense of comfort and reassurance that helped me to readjust. Music can be a wonderful healer, something that I had never realised before this trauma. It is at times like this that one finds inspiration in various ways that help one to survive. During those days it was most unusual to get a breakdown of a marriage, let alone all the scandal that went along with it. Bayly blew his top to all and sundry, accusing me of cruel treatment of his daughter, knocking her about, being almost bankrupt and anything that came into his head. He continued to be a regular attendant at his Methodist Church in his best clothes on a Sunday the rest of the week putting his so-called religion aside.

I kept a low profile during those terrible times, not wanting to go out, the terrible shame of it all, letting my family down, or so I thought, being quite a sensitive man, brought up to 'do unto others as you would expect them to do unto you.' That was my philosophy. I went through mental agony for a long time; several months went by before I realised that reconciliation was not going to happen. All correspondence was done through solicitors and after many months of frustration, I began to realise she had no intention of returning to me. My family was supportive, which was a great help to putting my life together again.

Eventually I forced myself out into the world again. People showed me quite a lot of sympathy. One local well-known man called Garfield Cowling visited me once during the early days of the separation and, having heard from Bayly his story, wanted to know from me if it was all true. During the conversation he told me how Marjorie would like to return to me, the information coming directly from her to him. I made no comment but immediately got in touch with my solicitor, who in turn got in touch with the inquiry agent, an ex-police sergeant who gave this fellow, Garfield Cowling, a visit to try to establish what was said to him and by whom. Evidence of this nature was very important to my pending case. I was suing both mother-in-law and father-in-law for enticement, taking away my wife and daughter against her wishes. I heard no further from this Mr Cowling. It could have been too hot for him to handle. By this time I was sorting myself out, deciding that whatever happened, if she voluntarily wanted to come back to me it would be only on my terms. I was now determined to get both my in-laws and my wife into court and speak under oath. Then I should get to know how Marjorie felt about our marriage after the long period of separation and stalemate.

During the time I was living alone, having established that Marjorie was not going to return, I employed various housekeepers and usually the husband to work on the farm. This suited me, as I was really like a lodger and was being looked after. I did have a few really nice, supportive people who I greatly appreciated. I did not have access to my child. Bayly would not in any circumstances allow me to see Janet; he did not want any maintenance from me for Marjorie or Janet. Those were his terms. I came to the conclusion it would be much better in the long-term if I did not have access to them, especially Janet. To have seen her would have had a further shattering impact on me and the hurt and pain would have reappeared. The solicitor advised me that I could get access to the child, but having had such a traumatic time with the family I decided that enough was enough and to keep well away. Going through this period of a few years of stress and agony made me quite determined and resolved to get Bayly at any cost.

I employed a Mr and Mrs Luscombe and their son Peter to help on the farm. Mr Luscombe was an ex-farmer, a good worker and reliable. Mrs Luscombe was very boastful and would travel by bus with her teenage son Peter quite regularly. She was a rather plump person and had full control over Harold, her husband. I used to feel sorry for him for he was often on his knees scrubbing the floors with her standing over him. Coming into the kitchen one day I observed him underneath the kitchen table washing the floor. When I asked why, his reply was it was his choice and he could do as he wished. In the meantime Mrs Luscombe was strutting around with dear Peter, who was a spoilt brat of about seventeen years of age. He wanted to be more involved with tractor work and he had a devious plan to get his own way - he decided to put sand into the fuel tank. It transpired that my tractor driver could not understand why the tractor kept stalling; yet Peter could manage to keep it going. Having two fuel tanks, one without sand, gave Peter the advantage. He was kept off all machinery after that affair. In the meantime Mrs Luscombe became very friendly with my wife and her family. This was a very awkward situation and she and her husband and their brat of a son eventually disappeared from the scene. Later on she was subpoenaed to appear at Court for the defence, but being an unreliable witness was not called to give evidence.

I also employed a Mr & Mrs Brock and their school age adopted daughter Jean. They were a super couple and their transport was a motorcycle combination. However after a few months they moved back to be nearer their old home.

Another couple I employed were a German ex-POW called Heinz and his little English wife Ethel. She was such a dear person, tried her best to please everyone, despite not being in the best of health, and in the evenings always wanted me to join her in her favourite game of 'Housey Housey'. Her sister would come on occasions to help her out. Illness took over and she was obliged to leave and return to her home in nearby Stratton with her sister. Heinz stayed on with me on the farm for a while, his wife eventually passed away and her father died at the same time, which meant that there was a double funeral at Stratton Church.

Heinz was a good worker but terribly temperamental. His father being ill in Germany he wanted some forward payment in lieu of wages to go out and visit him. I gave him

money for the trip and he went off to see his dad. On his return, because he owed me money and was expected to work to pay it off from his wages, he became so difficult that I sacked him rather than have the hassle maybe it was a useful ploy on his part.
A housekeeper called Nan came after them, stayed a short time and married Gerald; the farm worker and both then left the farm. There were also other employees who came to work for me both before and after the 1952 High Court case.

DURING the three year period, 1948- early1952, leading up to the case I made numerous visits to St Austell to see my solicitor Stanley Sampson. We spent many hours together, sometimes late into the evenings, to get to all the facts and put them together in a brief to present to the barrister for his attention. An enticement action was very difficult to prove, so they wanted sufficient evidence to present to the Court. I met the barrister, Hugh Park QC, with my solicitor on a couple of occasions and discussed some relevant points prior to the court case. It was at first going to be held at Winchester, but changed to Bodmin Assizes for convenience and cost. A civil action in the Chancery Division for enticement was quite a rare legal event, and this action between myself and Bayly and his wife for enticement, including trespass was beginning to attract local and national media interest.
Before the court action, a car with two men and an attractive woman called at the farm during a terrible snowstorm. They were very well dressed with a distinguished look. My immediate reaction before they even introduced themselves was that their visit must have been of importance, under such terrible weather conditions. The national press had printed something on the case and they were from a national newspaper. How was the action to be held? Were there any photos or relevant material they could use? All photos of mine had gone when Bayly stripped my home. Bayly had them all. I was quite civil to them but could show them nothing. They wanted to know about Bayly, I told them how they could find him, but didn't guarantee the reception that they would get.
A further meeting between myself, my solicitor and the QC, was arranged at the Royal Hotel, Bodmin to finalise a few points before the hearing the following day. The weather being foul I decided to stay at the hotel rather than be caught in a possible snowstorm and not be able to get to the hearing.
One witness Ashley Davey who was doing his National Service was recalled from Germany. He was with me at the time of Bayly taking the furniture. Doctor Hillier my GP was also to be called as a witness. This court action was going to be written up in the national papers and a number of journalists and photographers were present. There was no jury but Judge P L E Rawlings sat in judgement. Hugh Park, my barrister, was later to become Sir Hugh Park and a prominent judge. Mr Besley represented Bayly
I was apprehensive. At the entrance of the court I saw my three-year-old Janet running around in her little dress. She obviously did not know me but I knew the reason she was there was so they could try to wear me down. She later sat with them in the hearing.
I felt quite nervous in the witness box at first, but after being there for a while, being

questioned by my barrister, on many subjects I got my confidence and nothing would shake me. After that first day in the witness box being questioned chiefly by Mr Park, the following day it was the turn of the defendants' barrister, Mr Besley, to cross-examine me. He tried various manoeuvres to get the answer he wanted, and if it was not of his choice, he would go at the query another way hoping to confuse me. However my ordeal, after two days of examination and cross-examination, was coming to an end. The judge was taking notes, very alert, sometimes asking a few questions, putting the record straight. I had been warned by my counsel that I would be asked by the opposition: 'Do you want your wife back with you?' I had to say in reply: 'In view of what has happened in the past, I would have to consider that very carefully, sir.'

Thinking my ordeal was now getting to the end, Mr Besley, their barrister, asked me that very question. The judge at the time seemed to be half asleep but as soon as that question was put to me: 'Do you want your wife back with you?' he gave me a searching look. I could have been somewhat mesmerised by his looking at me in such a way, but I started to give my reply just uttering the pre-arranged words. The judge, after my reply, continued to look at me in a very searching manner for quite a long time. I realised the importance and the reason for this question. I had been away from my wife for three years, I was saying I wanted my wife back with me on the one hand, and on the other hand I am no longer interested in taking her back, hence my answer: 'In view of what has happened in the past I would have to consider that very carefully, sir.'

Bayly was brought to the witness box. I had waited a long time to get him there and it was a rather satisfying feeling. He proved a rather difficult witness, at times feigning deafness, leaning forward, hand behind the ears. The judge said: 'Bayly, are you hard of hearing?' 'No sir', says Bayly. 'Then answer the questions as they are put to you.' retorted the judge. No doubt this experience was unique to him, having to obey the stern and powerful voice of the judge who at times was showing his impatience toward him. 'Bayly, Bayly', he roared on one occasion: 'Stand to attention and answer the questions, do you understand?' Bayly, I recall jumped to attention and I became quite amused to see him being harassed and flustered. As certain questions were put to him he did not reply readily but kept trying to stall and hesitate in his speech. However the judge would have none of it and he was brought closer to the judge's box so that there were no further excuses for delaying the proceedings. I watched this bully of a man giving an exhibition of his attempts to fool the law but the law was having none of it in the courtroom were quite a few local people who were interested in the case.

The next person called was his wife. She did not last very long; she collapsed in the witness box and had to be taken out of the court. This held up proceedings but after half an hour they decided to continue and she was released by the agreement of both counsels. I was disappointed because she was the cause of many problems in our relationship and perhaps this was too easy a way out for her.

The next witness was my wife. I had waited three years to get her and her parents into court. She was asked many questions regarding our marriage and was questioned on her apparent suffering from depression, bordering on insanity, at that time, according to the doctor witness who spoke on her behalf. The big question I had waited so long for her to answer was eventually put to her as it turned out by her own counsel. When questioned regarding the circumstances of her leaving the marital home her reply was: 'I begged my father to take me away, I pleaded with my father that I wanted to leave him.' This was said by her under oath and left me in no doubt, after years of agony, of my next course of action, which of course would be a divorce. She would have to live with her conscience. I felt on having heard her speak these few words, a huge relief. She had had her day in court and had answered thus. I was now resolute; divorce would have to follow. The three lives affected by this terrible affair, mine and those of Marjorie and Janet were now set on a different course. However, she chose the road she wanted to follow and to me it was a great relief that it was all over.

After three days of sitting at Bodmin Judge Rawlings did his summing up at Plymouth Crown Court on Monday February 4th, I later learned that Judge Rawlings had consulted before the summing up with the Lord Chief Justice Goddard. This was a rare case under English Law. I can do no better than to quote the actual summing up of the judge. His words, not mine are the best ones available to close this very difficult chapter in my life.

In his summing up - regarding my wife:

Suffering a mild attack of depression, possible mild insanity, being convinced of the truth of her views but no foundation in them. She appeared normal until the child's birth. At the time of leaving she was bordering on a state of being useless, suffering from something delusive; and in my submission she was not a great value as a wife. '

As regards Mr Bayly:

He seriously infringed the rights of his son-in-law. His action in entering the farmhouse, removing furniture, standing on the table, pulling out the fittings from the walls and plaster, was clearly pre-arranged and planned. He was prepared to defend her cause, obviously devoted to his daughter and a strenuous defender of her rights as a married woman. A man of forceful and intemperate character. He is to return the canteen of cutlery, to pay £199 in damages for trespass, all the plaintiff's costs with the enticement action being dismissed.

As regards Mrs Bayly:

The husband is the dominant person in the household.

As regards myself:

A normal individual who always behaved in a very reasonable manner as a husband. A serious infringement of the plaintiff's rights had occurred. This has been a tragic story, a monstrous trespass.

There were many reports on the case in the local and national papers as an enticement action was a rare event in an English court, it has a very old lineage but in 1952 such a case aroused a lot of media interest. I refer you to some press headlines and some press cuttings below that were cut out and saved by my family.

No enticement, says judge, in case of—

WOMAN FULL OF GRIEVANCE

Express Staff Reporter: Plymouth, Monday

TWENTY-NINE-YEAR-OLD Marjorie Grigg was not enticed from her husband by her parents, it was ruled by Judge P. L. E. Rawlins today. So it was unnecessary, he said, to consider the "interesting problem which has been topical since the days of Solomon: What is the value of a good wife?"

MR. GRIGG   MRS. GRIGG
No reconciliation?

But the judge found that her father, 60-year-old Edward Bayly, of Braeside, Warbstow, Cornwall, "seriously infringed" the rights of his son-in-law, 6ft. Herbert William Grigg.

Mr. Bayly's action in entering Grigg's farmhouse at Fentrigan Farm, Warbstow, was "clearly prearranged and planned."

The judge awarded Grigg £150 damages against Mr. Bayly for trespass—plus £43 15s., the value of 35 head of poultry which were removed, £5 for detention of the poultry, and 5s. for the detention of a canteen of cutlery.

Awarded costs

Mrs. Bayly was dismissed from the case and awarded costs.

Judge Rawlins gave judgment at Plymouth. He had heard the case for three days last week at Bodmin County Court. He said this about—

THE HUSBAND: "I find on the evidence nothing in his conduct to reflect on his character as a husband, or man, or which, in law, would have justified his wife in leaving the matrimonial home."

THE WIFE: "She was quite normal until the birth of their child. Afterwards things of little importance assumed unjustifiable proportions in her mind.

"There is little doubt that she was full of a sense of grievance ably infected her parents with a similar sense."

HER FATHER was a man of "forceful character, obviously devoted to his daughter and a strenuous defender of her rights as a married woman."

The cutlery

Mr. Bayly, who wore black, well - polished leggings, and sat alone in court, handed over the canteen of cutlery as soon as the court rose. He has to bear three-quarters of the taxed costs of the action. He said afterwards: "I am thankful it has been proved that my wife and I never broke up our daughter's marriage. Reconciliation? Impossible. I should say."

Grigg left the court with his married sister. He carried the canteen of cutlery under his arm.

He said: "I shall not go on living at the farm. I am pleased that my character has been cleared."

The A40 gets a new face to please U.S.

By BASIL CARDEW

WHAT a sensible thing the Austin Motor Company has done today—giving its fantastically successful A40 car a new face, new body, and even a little more urge in the 1,200 c.c. engine.

For everywhere I went in the United States and Canada last year the Austin dealers told me: "Customers come in and say they want a new A40. But when we show them the same shape as they got three years ago, they say they want a new car."

Well, this A40 Somerset is a new car, from its Americanstyled front to its back bumper. There are new front grilles and radiator, a different type of bonnet, a new line of the mudguards which are swept through to the back. Price here £727 18s. 11d., including purchase tax.

And what a wonderful job the A40 Dorset and Devon saloons have done for their makers and for England.

The A40 was the first British light car of completely post-war design. In four and a half years more than 344,000 have been built, of which 77 per cent. have gone to world markets. Fantastically successful? Certainly. For it has earned £88,000,000 for Britain in export markets alone.

New liner for 1,093

The 13,875-ton liner Captain Cook sails from Glasgow tonight with 1,093 British emigrants to New Zealand.

Farmer Loses Enticement Claim Against In-laws

BUT GETS TRESPASS DAMAGES

By Daily Mail Reporter

WILLIAM HERBERT GRIGG, 31-year-old Cornish farmer, who yesterday lost his wife-enticement action against his parents-in-law, went back to Fentrigan Farm, Warbstow, last night with honour satisfied.

Giving his decision at Plymouth, Judge P. L. E. Rawlings awarded Mr. Grigg damages totalling £199 for trespass and the removal of certain goods against the father-in-law, Mr. Bayly.

"The important thing is that my character has been vindicated," Mr. Grigg told me later.

A mile away at Braeside Mr. Bayly, a 60-year-old retired farmer, who had also been ordered to pay three-quarters of the costs—probably another £150—was satisfied too. "I am not bothering about the trespass or the damages. I am quite happy now it has been proved that I did not wreck my daughter's marriage," he said.

During a three-day hearing at Bodmin Mr. Grigg alleged that his parents-in-law enticed his 29-year-old wife, Marjorie, to leave him, and that Mr. Bayly later led a raid on his farm, removing poultry and stripping the house of furniture.

'Tragic Story'

Yesterday Judge Rawlins described what he termed the principal actors in "this tragic story" thus:

Mr. Grigg: "A normal individual who always behaved in a very reasonable manner as a husband."

Mrs. Grigg: "A normal woman until the birth of her child. Then she suffered from a mild attack of depressive insanity. . . .

"She complained to her parents about her husband's hostile attitude towards her. I am satisfied she was convinced of their truth, but I am equally satisfied there was no foundation in fact."

Mr. Bayly: "A man of forceful character, obviously devoted to his daughter and a strenuous defender of her rights as a married woman."

Mrs. Bayly: "Her husband is the dominant person in the household."

No 'plague'

Referring to the claim for trespass and removal of certain property from Mr. Grigg's farm, the Judge said: "Although I do not subscribe to counsel's description of the descent on the plaintiff's farm as comparable to a 'plague of locusts,' I view it as a serious infringement of his rights and award him £159 damages."

He ordered a canteen of cutlery to be returned within 14 days, awarded a nominal 5s. for its detention, and assessed damages for the removal of 35 head of poultry at £43 15s., with another £5 for their detention.

Mrs. Bayly was dismissed from the case and awarded costs.

Daily Express 4th Feb 1952   *Daily Mail 4th Feb 1952*

74

In 1955 Bayly again was in breach of the peace and bound over for twelve months to keep the peace. In default he would go to prison for six months. I wished he had. He accused Mr Paynter, a cousin of mine, a county councillor, magistrate and local preacher, of intervening in the affairs of my enticement. He also threatened Paynter with a gun and offensive words.

Mr and Mrs Bayly are now both deceased, they died in old age several years ago. After the case my three-year-old daughter Janet, her mother and grandparents continued to live together as one family under one roof. Marjorie never remarried; she still carries my name and is still living at the same house with Janet, now 48 years of age and unmarried.

Janet I did not see for many years, but when she was about thirty she walked to the farm to see me and told me that she had not been allowed to contact me. For all those years she had only lived a mile away. She came to see me, to see the room in which she was born, she met and was made welcome by Margaret, my second wife and our four children. Janet has had her own share of bad luck and difficulties, she was a very bright and able pupil at school, she went to a local grammar school and was doing well at her job in Launceston when she suffered serious head injuries when her moped collided with a lorry that pulled out in front of her at a busy junction. Janet survived her injuries but although eventually fully recovered it took all of her twenties to get over her injury and when most youngsters of that age are out having fun, working and developing relationships Janet was not able to do these things because of her injuries.

Now in the evening of my years I do occasionally see her and we exchange birthday and Christmas greetings. I have recently gathered that she now has a boyfriend called Horace who is a widower and some years older than Janet. All I can do is hope that she finds happiness. I did hear from one source that her remarks were: 'Mother won't spoil this relationship as she did the last one.' Full marks, Janet. It has only been very recently in the last three or four years that Carole my partner for the past eight years has brought us together. It was at Carole's suggestion I should try to make amends for the years that passed with almost zero contact with my daughter. I believe Carole had a lot of empathy for the feelings of Janet in this matter because Carole had also not known her own natural mother, having been adopted at an early age.

PART TWO
ON MY OWN

There were several occasions or experiences that I recall. I remember the year was 1952 and I was going to a hunt ball at the Foster Hall, Bodmin, it was twenty miles away and I went unescorted. I had met some nurses from the local hospital who were living in nurse's accommodation. They were busy celebrating and I was invited to join them beforehand in their apartment to have some champagne. Not knowing the kick one gets from champers mixed with beer I was left rather legless. I tried to dance but collapsed on the floor. Taking me to the room adjoining the dance floor they took off my jacket and left me to sleep it off on the floor. As time wore on I awoke feeling chilled and all was quiet. Feeling the worse for wear I went to collect my car, the only one there. I stopped on the way home, had a nap and drove on again, arriving at the farm at about dawn when my resident workman was leaving the farmhouse, where he also lived with his wife, to start the day's work.

Another occasion I remember of over indulgence. Launceston market was held on a Tuesday, it was quite a large market in the district, mainly for fatstock. It died out some ten years ago and is now a car park and shops. I remember making arrangements that I would be returning early from market to do all the yard work myself. Having met a number of associated buddies in the pubs left me the worse for wear. After some time and having over-indulged in liquor, I decided to return. On getting to the farm, feeling very tired, I decided to take a nap.

When I woke in the middle of the night there was pandemonium, about thirty cows were roaring to be milked, a further twenty to thirty calves were wanting their feed, two hundred pigs waiting for their evening meal, and a number of single suckled cows waiting to feed their calves. Getting up in the middle of the night in a stupor and having to face that lot taught me a lesson for the future, not to over indulge in midday drinking. I will add that two hundred pigs all screaming and the cows and calves roaring to be fed and milked was an experience that I would like to forget.

Me (left) and Brother (right) c1953

It was Christmas Eve 1953. Tony Raspa, an ex Italian POW who helped me on the farm joined me that evening and we arranged to go out for a few drinks. After a long session he decided to stay with friends whom he had met that evening. I had previously bought from a Doctor Rawson his Flying Standard saloon car HCV 123 from Tintagel (the car being well known in that area, my name was and still is HCV 123). Arriving back from this night out very late I got as far as the farm entrance; the car stalled and I could not get it started I decided to leave the car just outside the farm entrance by the parish road. The farm drive was half a mile and I staggered towards the farmhouse. On arriving a party was on, so I temporarily joined them. The following day, Christmas Day, I had arranged to go to my mum and dad's home at St Mabyn for dinner. John and his wife Olive were living in the farmhouse helping with the running of the farm and at the same time looking after me, cooking, washing etc, as I was then divorced.

When the morning arrived Olive had great difficulty in waking me. Eventually getting my act together and walking to the farm entrance to get to the car, I could not distinguish it as it had changed its colour to brown. It was completely burnt out, only a shell remained. The interior was just metal and springs, dashboard, steering wheel, tyres flat, little pools of solder on the floor. My dad's hobnail boots, having been repaired were burnt to a cinder. Walking back to the farm, John and Olive lent me their car to drive to my parents' house. Needless to say I did not have any dinner and I didn't feel much in the Christmas spirit. At least I did not as a bachelor farmer suffer a Christmas as bad as that of a foolish fellow called Sargeant. I took some grass keep at Townlake, near Horsebridge from a Mr Sargeant. A single man and not a very good farmer, he had also partly let his farmhouse to a large family who eventually more or less took it over and in due course he was no longer master of his own house. I recall hearing of the story of him calling for his Christmas dinner by knocking on the door, he was not allowed in but he was presented with the remains of the turkey, mostly bones, which he accepted and had to eat.

IT WAS early December, the year I cannot remember but it was the time of the annual Smithfield Show at Earls Court, London and a group of us decided to go. My friend a local farmer Clifford Orchard, his workman, 'Growler' of eighteen years service who had never been to London before and Dennis who farmed in partnership with his brother Clifford. The heavy autumn work was complete and a little relaxation was needed. Going by car to Exeter St David's station we boarded the train and we were on our way, arriving at Paddington station and then getting on the underground to Piccadilly Circus, within easy reach of our pre-booked Regent Palace Hotel.

Coming from the country we felt we were the boys come to the big city speaking in our broad Cornish accents. We felt we could handle any situation. Growler was a sturdy well-built guy with a raucous voice, heavy beard and thick black hair.. The underground train halted at the platform, the automatic doors opened and Growler was aghast at the crowds pushing and rushing, getting inside, finding standing room only and the doors being automatically closed. In a little while the carriage had more seating available, which we took advantage of. All the passengers were sitting and reading their papers. Growler, in his raw, inexperienced rustic manner blurted out loud enough for all to hear: 'All the fuckers here seem to be eating their papers. Ain't um got nort else to do?' That remark being well and truly received, the papers immediately dropped and all eyes were centred on the speaker we were on our way, a good opening.

My 72nd birthday party with Cliff Orchard (1992)

Having settled into our rooms at the Regent Palace, Growler always keeping in close proximity, not being used to so many people, the lift, or the plush surroundings, we decided to go to a restaurant for a meal. Hiring a taxi we found a highly respectable restaurant, tables well furnished, waiters all suitably dressed. Lights and furnishing very plush and ladies and gentlemen were well dressed and this posh restaurant was very busy. We were escorted to a table for four people. Chairs were pulled out and seating appropriately arranged. The menu being presented, our orders were duly taken. This was a completely new world for Growler, and it was quite amusing to watch his reactions. Later on having eaten our fill, the bill was presented and after going over the details, we called the waiter to our table to query a few points. Dennis started the enquiry with his brother Clifford in support; Growler and I sat back in our chairs and observed the confusion. It went on for some time, voices being raised in the process, causing a little uneasiness within the restaurant. The headwaiter came and tried to placate and make an attempt to meet the bill halfway. Having proved that we had sufficient money to pay the bill in cash, the management was becoming quite uneasy because of the disturbance being caused by these West Country lads over the bill not being properly itemised and priced. Police were mentioned but we knew that would be no advantage to their good name. The management accepted a very small payment and were pleased to see us away. The argument was about a mistake on the number of bread rolls.

I well remember some years previously when going to the show with a group of farmers by coach from the Wadebridge area, getting to the outskirts of London, we ran into one of those fogs known as 'pea-soupers', or smog. We took turns to run slowly in front of the bus with a torch to guide the coach driver along. It was a complete blackout, you could not see more than a couple of yards. It appeared as though you were completely isolated, houses were not seen, street lights were there but of no use. Arriving eventually at our hotel we found that everything you touched made you filthy, we were even coughing up black phlegm. To sit on a toilet seat left you with a black backside.

The animals at the show, being so fat, had difficulty in their breathing because of the smog, and had to be drenched with beer or Guinness to help their congested lungs. I think some of the animals died through the stress.

We had some amusement when in the big city. Buying a toy dog, one that would bark and go forward in a jumping action, caused a lot of fun on a busy London street. Setting it up with my friend, we decided to put the dog into action, barking and jumping forward, with us shouting orders to 'go. A large crowd gathered, probably thinking that we were a couple of nut cases.

It was probably in the early 1950's that I made my first of several visits to Smithfield Show, which occurs every year in early December at Earls Court. On this occasion I prearranged to meet a good friend Stewart Turner at my hotel in London one evening. We had a few beers together and after a little while Stewart retired for an early night, as he had to be at the show early the following morning. Shortly after he left I was approached by a man and we entered into a conversation. He was tall, well presented in his early twenties and spoke with an American accent. I at first being naturally on my guard with a complete stranger eventually entered into a deeper conversation. His proposition was to go to the nightclub 'Churchill's'. I had heard that this was an up-market, respectable club, but had never been there. I did not have sufficient money on me to afford expensive London nightclubs, but he was prepared to take me along with him. I insisted he accepted what money I had on me, and he eventually accepted. Calling a taxi we set off about 11pm. On getting to 'Churchill's' we were met by the uniformed doorman and eventually shown to a table. We took our seats and they offered us a bottle of champagne together with a couple of hostesses to keep us company, and a large packet of cigars. The lights were dimmed and a cabaret was in progress, all very exciting for me. Two girls joined us and my chorus girl was attentive and talkative telling me she originated from London and during the war years she had been evacuated to a farm in Wales and spent a few years as a land girl mainly potato picking.

We had something in common to talk about and the evening became quite interesting. The cabaret over, dancing with her and asking if I could have another date while I was in London, she said if she was seen leaving the club with a client she could get sacked. We continued dancing well into the night with me becoming quite merry and enjoying the caviar and champagne, after all my new American friend was picking up the bill.

He was a traveller for Ford Motors from Detroit, their European representative, spending his time in various European countries selling Ford motors. He was returning to the USA the following day and he told me that being given expenses money from the firm, he didn't want to take it back with him, hence my very good fortune. As the night wore on we were joined by a further group from International Harvester Ltd who were exhibiting at Smithfield. All in all it was an illuminating and exciting evening, one that stayed with me for a long time. I realised that my lifestyle could in no way compare to theirs. I realised that their world compared to mine, although enticing, was an artificial one, my world was the real world and I would not want to change it for theirs. It was time for us to leave Churchills, saying our goodbyes and the friendly generous American duly paid the evening's entertainment bill for me of £75. I had never realised that such an amount could be spent in a single night out on the town. I probably compared the cost of it all to the number of cows or tons of wheat I could have purchased for the same amount. A taxi took us to our respective hotels, with my friend Stewart incredulous and jealous of my good fortune when I recounted the story to him the following day.

Later that week I had been invited by Stewart to a Masonic Installation at the Temple in Great Queen Street, London through our friends Ted and Mary Dunstan who kept the Kings Arms at Holsworthy. It was a relation of theirs, a solicitor from Brighton who was being installed as the Worshipful Master. The Queen Street venue is a massive building made up of a large number of independent lodges. The lodge that we attended consisted of solicitors, barristers, judges and anyone connected with the Courts. I was already a Master Mason from my King Arthur Lodge in Tintagel, and Stew was a Past Worshipful Master, which qualified us to be amongst the gathering of the clan. Suitably clad in our regalia we watched the five judges arrive to take their places amongst the high officers. The working of this lodge was most impressive and done in a style that suited the occasion.

After the installation of the new Worshipful Master for the year ahead, we proceeded to the Connaught Rooms in the same building to have our banquet. What particularly impressed me were the after-dinner speeches given by these professional, talented orators, who kept the audience spellbound. It was a unique occasion and a privilege to have been invited. We were invited the following day to see the Grand Temple and Museum. On opening the massive bronze doors of the entrance to the Grand Temple I was awestruck by the beauty and size. The organ was playing the carol 'Silent Night'. I felt as though I was moving into another world, especially with the acoustic effect of the music throughout the Temple.

On another evening I was having a quiet beer at the public bar of my hotel when I was surprised to see a Launceston businessman Freddie Smith who owned a large garage. Freddie (now long gone) joined me at the bar and invited me to join him for a meal at Simpsons, which had a good reputation for high-class food, which was plentiful and presented in style. The barons of beef and other juicy meats were on a trolley, brought to the table and carved to our requirements. Having indulged, Freddie decided to meet his pal Stan whom I also knew very well. The three of us went to a strip show. Stan, who was a farmer in his early fifties, had told me way back in our local that he had a problem – he had confided that his sex urge was dormant or gone. He was a pleasant character, a bald and fairly sturdy man who would ramble on and on. Being of a genuine and serious nature he would not hesitate to enlarge upon his private life in conversation. In the environment of the strip club with the strippers doing their act, after a while Stan, in his congenial way, leaned across to me, saying: 'Bill, there's hope, I feel something perking up.' 'Oh, good - sshhh, be quiet,' says I. The show over, we had a backstage drink with some girls, which got poor Stanley in a right conflict with himself.

The following evening we went to the Windmill ('We never close' was the motto of the theatre during the war) and afterwards called at the Windmill Club, which we found quite entertaining with the women's low-cut dresses and protruding boobs. We tried to distinguish who was who in the dimmed atmosphere. It had its advantages.

Another time I experienced something completely new and different from anything I had ever experienced in my sheltered country life. Standing on the steps of Eros in Piccadilly Circus one evening on my own, I was impressed by all the activity that was going on around me, traffic, taxis, buses, cars, all roaring along, horns being blown, the neon lights flashing. I was completely awe struck. I was then approached by a short, well-dressed man aged about thirty with a beard, he started chatting to me and told me he was playing a role in the film or play 'Rob Roy'. He began to ask why I was alone. I was rather naive and consequently quite disgusted when I was suddenly asked to spend the night with him. I walked off.

On another occasion, going to my hotel room via the lift to the sixth floor I was approached by a gentleman to join him for a coffee in his room. Not giving this much thought, I decided to join him. Pulling his chair toward me, he began to fondle my knees. I immediately left him in no doubt that he was with the wrong man, he withdrew and our acquaintance was short-lived. I left the room still smarting from this episode.

MORE COUNTRY CHARACTERS

Just before Christmas 1954, the house had to be updated, because early the following year I was going to be married for the second time. Tom Peniston the builder, Bill Warren and myself set to work. Bill was my farm worker, a short fellow, thickset, a walk like a rocking horse not helped by his bow legs. He had a funny squeaky under-developed voice and a unique laugh, his teeth were few and protruding, but he was a conscientious worker.

We had a busy time altering the shape and character of some of the rooms. The dairy and pantry adjoining the kitchen were made into one room. It was my intention to change it into a kitchen and the present kitchen would be our lounge. The granite trundle which my mum used for salting and curing the pig was put outside (it is now used as a flower trough). The Delabole slate slab benches were all taken down and removed. Cupboards and kitchen furniture were made by a local craftsman; a cooker was installed backing up to the chimney on the opposite side of the wall. The clome oven was taken out regrets are still with me. They call it progress; yes, it was, but we should stop and think of the historical values and emotional attachments to certain features in our homes before discarding them. The seducing modern view is that you have to keep up with the times otherwise you will get left behind.

After working away like beavers for some time we decided to break for lunch, Bill was telling us how he could carry his beer and we all had quite a few drinks together. Lunch extended well into the afternoon. Back at work we decided we would clear away the loose rubble that had accumulated. Having loaded the wheelbarrow it was Bill's lot to take it outside to a dumping area in the farmyard. A little unsteadily, he attempted to lift and move the barrow forward. This was successful for a few yards, then weaving around suddenly the whole lot collapsed in a heap. He picked himself up looking rather ludicrous and pressed on towards the tip. He left the wheelbarrow on the top of the tip and walked unsteadily to a barn and lay down in the straw beside a sleeping sow that recently had a litter of pigs. It was rather cold, being around Christmas time. Bill was well and truly drunk.

I got an old coat to cover him with and found that he was asleep cuddled up close to the sow's large breasts. This was quite amusing to see, the sow obviously enjoyed having her breasts stimulated. Surprisingly the sow stayed asleep and on the odd occasion the sow would grunt and move its whole breasts towards the sleeping Bill. The dog in the farmyard was barking and somehow knew that there was something very unusual going on. Groceries were delivered monthly by van from Launceston. That afternoon the delivery man arrived with our month's supply, saw the pair asleep and decided that living in the country area was not so monotonous. Time was moving on. Bill was expected back home as he was supposed to be going to a Christmas party that evening. Trying to wake him was no easy task, however Tom Peniston and I eventually succeeded in getting him indoors, putting on some strong coffee and feeding him with a spoon, some he took in, some he wasted. After quite a long time he came around and was helped into Tom's car to take him home about four miles away by Tom who lived nearby. I gathered later that his wife had left for the party without him. Bill arrived home with Tom helping him to the door. Tom made a quick get away not knowing that Bill's wife had already left. Tom did however see Bill push the front door open and fall into the passageway, calling: 'Darling, I'm home at last. Darling, where are you?'

DURING some winters a local farmer's son, Tommy Diniss, did some ploughing for me. He had an iron wheeled Oliver 90 tractor and a three-furrow plough. The field in question was quite wet and there was a lot of rushes and long marsh grass. Tommy was a local character, well known by all, with a good vocabulary and a good general knowledge, an expert on what he knew, especially the world of the bee. I will return to this later. To bury the rushes successfully he had a heavy chain dragging alongside the mouldboard of the plough, as the deep furrow was being turned over so the rushes were buried beneath. Large stones and boulders were a problem and that was his speciality. Seeing a large stone, he would immediately descend and, with pick and shovel, dig until he had brought the stone to the surface. This used to infuriate me as, as I had told him previously, he was paid to plough, not to dig out stones. In the long term I now thank him for what he did. No longer was the plough hitting large rocks hidden beneath the surface, which broke the ploughshares and twisted the plough. The field with rushes was called 'Lower Long Park' approximately six acres, with a heavy type of soil, a few large exposed spar rocks, which we eventually broke up. However while Tommy was ploughing he hit a very large flat stone, bringing the tractor to a standstill, almost stalling the engine; not too difficult, especially with iron wheels. He got out the chain, pulling at this large rock with the tractor and making for the river bank at the far end of the field. Away he went, stone following the tractor, Tommy looking behind all the time. He was getting near to a lot of undergrowth, small bushes, furze and young trees. He was still not looking ahead but fascinated by the huge stone in tow and still he carried relentlessly on towards danger. I began to run, shouting and swinging my arms at him, to no avail. He entered the undergrowth, bushes being thrown aside by the tractor, stone still in transit behind, Tommy out of sight still in his swivel seat, the tractor and stone by this time out of my sight. Running to the spot I was relieved to see that he had stopped inches from the edge of the riverbank and not a bit concerned.

Tommy was a great character. He was in his younger days a motor cycle enthusiast. He used to ride at Exeter Speedway in races as well as entertaining the crowds with daring stunts. He was eventually banned from the stadium for riding his bike on the wall of a bridge. His favourite bike was a Rudge Ulster or Whitworth. His mother, father and Cyril, his brother, lived quite close to our farm. His father and Tommy could not agree and they would go for weeks without any acknowledgement or contact whatsoever. His mum was a lovely lady and used to attend whist drives with my mum at times. Cyril, his brother, had an illness, which stayed with him all his life; he died soon after his mother and his dad died soon after. Tommy tried farming but did not last very long. He would ask my advice, but would not take much notice. Buying machinery was his pet subject and eventual downfall.

An agricultural merchant calling to see him one day was amazed to see a note on the door saying, 'Anyone found on these premises will be shot on sight.' You can use your own imagination as to what move the rep made! Tommy was an unusual but ultimately harmless character.

I remember very clearly the first time I met Tommy. He was quite a few years older than me. As a young boy dad sent me to the cobbler, a Mr Charles Prout, who was also our postman. He regularly walked several miles to each farm to deliver the post. (One bad winter he was only able to walk to our farm by coming over the gates and hedges because of the heavy snowfalls and the deep drifts.) I remember the time as a youngster having arrived at his cobbler's shop about three miles away on my newly-bought bicycle for which I had saved my precious pennies, I entered the shop. Mr Prout was busy. Sitting on the form was this other man unknown to me. He began to ask me questions, finding out where I lived and my name. He now knew the way I would be going home. He told me of a weird animal that had been seen crossing my homeward route. He called it a 'Uzeka', whatever that meant. I was at a loss. He however was convincing and left me with a dilemma. How could I avoid that particular route on my way home, I could not go a different way for it was getting dark. As I got nearer the spot I was thinking of this terrible hairy bear-like animal, the 'Uzeka'. Pushing my bicycle up the hill and putting on a brave face, with bated breath, I waited for 'Uzeka' to attack. I passed the dreaded spot, trying hard to discipline myself for the unexpected, but nothing happened. The 'Uzeka' was nothing but one of Tommy's tall stories.

Tommy and I had a lifelong friendship although we did not see so much of each other in his later years. He moved away to live in Launceston in his old age with a widow called Ethel. Tommy had farmed close to me at his own farm Tredown. His wife suddenly left him one day taking their four young children and went back to the Midlands. I believe she originated from Coventry. Tommy held on for several years, trying to make a living out of a difficult wet farm. He was well known and respected for his bees. He was an expert beekeeper, he was mad about bees. He became quite a celebrity in the bee world. He also became very friendly in his old age with my eldest son Trevor and he too for a time kept several hives with great encouragement from Tommy. In his eighties he would appear on TV occasionally demonstrating his beekeeping skills with nothing more than a cigarette to calm his beloved bees. To the viewers he must have seemed rather crazy with no veil or gloves, just his love and enthusiasm for bees. I was a bearer at his funeral in 1991. He died in an old people's home.

FENTRIGAN FARM

My life as a farmer was of course at Fentrigan Farm. This was the sole source of my livelihood and for better or worse these few hundred acres just north of Bodmin Moor was the fate and the hand that I had been dealt and I farmed it as best as I could. At it's highest point it is approximately 800 feet above sea level. It commands a spectacular view of the sea including on a clear day a view of Lundy Island, Bude Bay and Hartland Point. Exmoor, Bodmin Moor and Dartmoor can also be seen. The farm is rather exposed to the south westerlies and the land is an easy working and free-draining loam especially in and around the farmstead. The underlying stone can be easily cut and shaped, even by a saw, and on being exposed hardens in texture. Warbstow Church was built by freestone hauled from small quarry on the farm, and North Petherwin and Week St Mary churches were also built from this same stone in the Norman times. Fentrigan has a fairly bleak northerly aspect and slopes down to approximately 450 feet above sea level. It is about five miles from the north Cornish coastline. In 1959 an adjoining farm called Trenannick came up for sale. My new local bank manager did not approve of my interest in buying this additional land, and made life difficult for me, but as it adjoined my own farm I had to have a go.

My father when he died in November 1955 left Fentrigan Farm to me apart a small annuity of fifteen pounds a year each to my brother and three sisters. Possibly because of my first marriage and the trauma of the divorce and the court case he was not sure and undecided what to do with the farm at his death. He had a heart problem and he had been ill for some time but when I married again in 1955 he left the farm to me in his will I could therefore offer some collateral to the bank, but it was not interested in lending. Here was a wonderful opportunity as I saw it of expanding the farm, I had two young sons and I was not going to let the opportunity slip by. It would add 240 acres of mainly flat or south-facing fertile land, capable of growing and producing good crops and livestock, together with a new four-bed bungalow (with a 20-year agricultural restriction), a farmhouse and farm buildings.

At the time I had great difficulty in raising the finance, I was doing it against the National Provincial Bank's wishes and the very morning I was supposed to have paid the deposit, I had a short and sharp letter from the bank with their opinion, which really upset me. I had to be careful what I was doing because the bank wouldn't support me but I needed them to continue supporting my overdraft facility. The owner was a Mr Brian Roberts of London. He was a nice gentleman and the night editor of the Sunday Express. £2,500 was on mortgage from Dr Thompson who some years since had a practice at our local town. Through Peter Kivell of the land agents Kivells I received some extra time and support from the seller who was a real gentleman about the matter and didn't pressure me. Wesley Smith (my brother-in-law) and I eventually bought the whole 240-acre farm between us with a farmhouse, a bungalow and farm buildings for £7,500. We then split the purchase between us. I got the bungalow and the major part of the land. He took the rest. Many years later in 1983 I sold the bungalow and ten acres of land for £45,000

When my father took over the farm from his uncle in about 1922 it was in a bad way. Father did what he could in the following years to make improvements but money was tight and he struggled. Mother did her bit with selling eggs, poultry, and butter and we children worked the farm as well when not at school. It was the war that really brought Fentrigan back into a productive farm. Up until that time we only grew ten or fifteen acres of cereals mainly oats and barley. Father would hand-sow the fields and spread manure on the fields using a prong from the back of a cart. We kept some sheep, Devon Longwools, they would rather die than live, and they would just give up when having a difficult lambing. The first thing I did when I started farming on my own accord was to get rid of the Longwools and have some hill-born cross breeds. We also kept the traditional Red Devon (Ruby) cattle and some Angus cattle. I made changes here too. I wanted to get into milk.

I wanted Ayrshires, which was new for Cornwall. I was the first person I believe in Cornwall to introduce them. They were dual purpose, good for milking and reasonable as a beef breed. I thought they were better than Friesans as you could keep three Ayrshires compared to two Friesans on the same acreage. I purchased a number of in-calf Ayrshire heifers of good quality from an agent who used to import them from Scotland. They were of a good conformation, producing quality milk and of a hardy constitution and suited my farm for some years. Unfortunately they had horns which were a nuisance, they had to be removed by injecting the base with some local anaesthetic and sawing them off. A very bloody and messy task but ultimately successful and desirable for the future welfare of the animals. Tuberculosis (TB) was common in cattle in those days. Only two local farms had TB-free herds and I could see that TB eradication in herds was the next big thing in milk and beef production. Eric Sloman and I were the first two farmers in our immediate district to bring in TB testing throughout our whole herds. The test was called the double intradermal test. A vet had to make two injections into the skin of the neck an antigen and an antibody and then re-visit three days later and measure the thickness of the swelling. If the thickness of the swelling was above a certain limit then the animal had to be injected again and the process repeated. Failure a second time was a strong indicator that the animal was TB infected. We had no cattle crushes in those days to assist in retaining the cattle; it was done by herding as many cattle as you possibly could into a small enclosure, usually a small building with solid stone walls.

It was difficult work. The vet had to be present to do the necessary neck jabs, we had to identify the animal by ear tag numbers and hold them by using a noose or by twisting their neck sideways and this all had to be repeated when measuring the swelling on the neck after a few days. It was stressful both to man and beast without the convenience of a cattle crush. It was soon after this initial round of testing that I bought a cattle crush.

I clearly remember a particular veterinary surgeon coming to the farm to carry out the tuberculosis tests He was from the Ministry of Agriculture. I noticed that he would quietly approach the animal, look into its eye and it seemed as though the animal was hypnotised. He was a fairly elderly gentleman with a Scottish accent, greying hair and not too tall, it was quite impressive how he used this technique, thus making life a lot easier for all.

Any cattle that proved to be reactors had to be destroyed. A TB reactor would cause problems and delay the movement of animals from and to the farm. After ninety days of restrictions further tests were carried out and if the animals passed, the sale and movement of cattle could return to normal. However if the TB problem persisted, as it did on some farms, this caused an embarrassment to the finances and the breeding and rearing of stock. It was not easy to plan under these circumstances.

There were certain areas of the British Isles where testing for TB did not yet apply and these areas were selling large numbers of newly calved cows to the West Country. Monthly local farm sales were held, with these imported recently calved or about to calve cows fetching high prices. These cows were eventually tested and it was shown that large numbers of them were infected. This was not very satisfactory and not appreciated except by the few who made large profits from this venture.

I had also bought an Ayrshire bull, wild and really quite unmanageable. He had to be kept tethered at all times and he used to make an almighty roaring and bellowing every time a car came into the farmyard. This bull was very ill tempered and I did not enjoy the dangerous task of putting the bull to the cow. This was done by putting a staff to the nose ring and then untying him and controlling this huge beast at all times by inflicting pain on him through the ring. It was fraught with difficulties especially when trying to control him when mounting and servicing the tethered cow. When the business was done the bull was taken back to the stall and tied as before, however on one occasion, when I was alone, the bull attempted to charge and caught me. Luckily I got away and after a short time I fainted probably through delayed shock. It was soon after this lucky escape that I decided this bull was too dangerous and had to go. I got in touch with the local abattoir, a lorry was sent to collect and after some difficulty with loading, I was pleased to see him go. Inquiring from the abattoir about the carcase, I was informed that the carcase was of no use for human consumption as the bull was full of TB. This I refused to accept as I had recently obtained a TB-free herd status. I visited the abattoir and seeing the carcase I had to agree. I later learned from the vet that very infrequently an animal with a lot of TB can indeed pass the test.

One year I took by train a number of Ayrshire cows to Reading market in company with another local farmer, Murray Hurst, a Canadian, who had an attractive wife, whose father was 'Gimcrack', the racing correspondent for a national daily paper. Murray was tall, rather thin, about thirty years of age and with not much farming experience but exceptionally good fun to be with. Our cows arrived at Reading looking rather dirty from their long journey in the cattle trucks and had to be washed down and groomed prior to the auction. The sale was not too satisfactory and some of the cows were brought back to the farm. Murray and I stayed at a hotel and I remember trying out the flavours of the top shelf. This was a new experience for me and that night I nearly choked to death on my own vomit. Murray was perhaps more acclimatised to this type of drinking and did not appear to get so drunk. When we recovered from our hangovers we drove back to Cornwall and to the local station to collect the returned cows. Murray was a good friend. Launceston market day on a Tuesday was not to be missed. This was a weekly social gathering, Murray and other friends and I would meet up at the White Hart. He was quite a fellow.

BUILDING THE FUTURE

WHEN I first took over the farm I was fired up with enthusiasm and like most young newly-weds I was ambitious for the future. The fields had to be made larger for machinery. It was no use having field sizes of four, five, six acres. Hedges often riddled full of rabbit holes had to be bulldozed away. The horse and cart days were thankfully gone. There was a price however to be paid for removing the hedges, less shelter for livestock in rough weather, no windbreaks to prevent excessive snowdrifts. In a blizzard the farm lane, below the level of the enlarged fields, would rapidly fill with drifts cutting us off from the outside world, at one time in 1947-48 for eight weeks and again in the big freeze of 1962 and in subsequent blizzards in more recent years.

In the late fifties and early sixties I put up large new farm buildings with wide clear spans, built concrete yards and implement sheds. I put in water and electricity; I built extra barns to store hay and straw. There were so many improvements done to accommodate more livestock through the winter and to make life generally easier. Ewes could now be housed for lambing. Losses were high when lambing out of doors because of frequent bad weather and no shelter. The large barn covering approximately twelve thousand square feet was adaptable being used for grain storage and drying at harvest time. I bought an Air Force Nissen hut from the disused aerodrome at Davidstow; re- erected it on the farm and filled it with pigs for fattening. Fattening of pigs gave an acceptable profit margin, which encouraged me to erect a much larger piggery for 200 pigs. Timber and materials were bought from demolition sites in Plymouth, and with local farm labour to build it, it cost about a thousand pounds.

Serving Harvest Tea

Fentrigan Farm 1955

It was completed about the time of the birth of Trevor my eldest son born in December 1955. My dear dad died the month before and I dearly wished that he had been alive to see his grandson. To fill this new piggery I had to purchase 200 eight-week old pigs at a cost of approximately a tenner each from Launceston market. To feed them cost another £10 each so the total investment was £4,000. The moment I had 200 fat pigs ready for the sale, the Ministry of Food decided that they would not be buying any more on open contract and all pigs were to be sold on the open market. This came as a bombshell, pigs selling previously at approximately £22-£24 each were down to £12-£14 each. Pigs were graded and fat measurements taken, and if they did not meet the required specification they would be drastically cut in price. I ultimately sent this first batch to the Totnes and Bridgwater factories of Harris bacon and I travelled there too, to argue the prices paid and the fat measurements. Having lost money on my first consignment, I had no alternative than to carry on but I had to do a complete re-appraisal of my feeding and breeding technique if I intended to make a profit and recover my losses. I bought as before young weaned farrows, feeding them up to six score porkers. I drastically reduced the feed bill by buying whey from Davidstow cheese factory and collected cooked offal from Plymouth for a short while. My feed bills still amounted to approximately £1,000 per month (a lot of money in those days). I also wanted to breed my own weaners. I went to a breeder near Lands End and bought four saddleback gilts and I bought a large white boar. I also purchased several sows and their litters from the markets until I had built up a breeding herd of approximately 35 sows. The market dictated I had to be a low cost producer. I bought a quantity of secondhand railway sleepers, laying ten of them up against a stone field hedge side by side with a small entrance, enough for a sow to enter, and this covered with some old corrugated galvanised steel sheets, was what I used to farrow the sows in. Each pen had an outside area, controlled by an electric fence.

This idea was very cheap and highly successful with hardly any losses either in summer or winter. It was amazing during severe weather conditions how the sow with her litter would keep extremely warm. These saddleback sows were producing approximately ten farrows each and it helped towards the supply of weaners for fattening. I was still having to buy weaners from the markets. During this time I was feeding all pigs to porker weight and sending a lorry of porkers per week to a factory near Helston. It took a long time to recoup those early losses and I had the extra investment of building up my breeding stock. As time progressed I gradually moved from producing porkers to selling off eight-week farrows by contract at so much per pound. This proved to be quite profitable. Rearing the farrows under such natural conditions with access to grass, earth and minerals etc, they were very healthy. All piglets had to be wormed and the males castrated by holding the piglet against the body by the back legs, exposing the small testicles. With a quick cut of the razor blade and then dosing the wound with salt the castration was done in seconds. Of course there was a lot of resistance and squealing from the few-days-old piglet.

❖   ❖   ❖

Me at home 1960

IN ABOUT 1960 with a young family of two sons and a daughter Bridget who was born that year I diversified into other farming activities. I decided to get out of milk. I had had enough of being tied to the cow's tit twice a day, 365 days a year. I wanted to do other things. I had already started doing some agricultural contracting work and I must have been employing about five or six farm workers at this period. I found it convenient and cost effective to employ and integrate the labour towards other projects. I already had one lorry for hauling sand from Padstow to farms so my thinking was to set myself up as a hay and straw merchant. This would require more lorries and drivers. Hay and straw, especially the straw, would be purchased off the field in East Anglia and the Home Counties during harvest time and hauled back to customers in Devon and Cornwall.

To get started in this venture I went to Rush Green Motors in Hertfordshire with Walter Aldridge and son Brian who knew a thing or two about lorries. We were in the market for a couple of lorries. Rush Green Motors could be best described as a lorry graveyard annexed to a small dairy farm deep in the Hertfordshire countryside. There were literally scores of secondhand lorries covering several acres being stored one on top of the other. During the Great Train Robbery, which happened in the vicinity, the police turned the place upside down but did not find anything. Alsatians were plentiful, chained at various points within the scrapyard.

They were a bunch of honest rogues. The big chief had his Roller and small aircraft and of course a runway to go with it. A caravan was the office as is usual in these types of premises and we negotiated with a most charming sales negotiator called Sandy. Having purchased a couple of lorries for cash, their only terms, we drove away to pre-arranged farms and loaded them with hay for delivery back home in the West Country.

After a few weeks, not being satisfied with one of the lorries, I decided to go back to Rush Green Motors and change this unreliable lorry if possible. Arriving early one morning at the adjoining house to the lorry park I was met by an 8ft fence and about a dozen crazy Alsatians trying to get out at me. My only choice was to wait until someone came. No one seemed to be at home. I heard a machine working at the rear. I cautiously walked around the back to investigate only to meet a muscular bouncer who didn't give me a chance to explain. In his own forthright terms he told me to 'hop it' or words to that effect and to come back later. Not so much charm on this visit I thought. Now they had my money their promise of allowing a change of lorry if unsatisfied after a trial period seemed rather empty.

Apparently their terms for visitors were completely rural. No visitors until after the cows were milked and that wasn't likely until 10am. I had to be patient and it eventually paid off. They allowed a change of lorry and I was on my way.

Having the lorries meant employing more staff. I did some driving as well and I had one trustworthy long-term driver called Brian Aldridge who lived in the nearby hamlet of Trelash. I also needed another driver and over the five or six years of running this haulage business I must have got through several drivers who never proved to be as reliable or honest as I expected. I remember one such fellow who was with me for a few years called

Bernie Peerless. Now Bernie had a bit of a colourful past as regards a few run-ins with the law. I am not sure if he had ever done time, but he came with a good reference from someone well known to me so I gave him a chance as a farm labourer and lorry driver. One day he was bringing a load of straw back from up country when I got a phone call in the middle of the night from the police.

The lorry and all the straw had caught fire on the A30 at Lewdown. The road was completely blocked, traffic had to be diverted by the police and the fire brigade had no chance as the straw was well alight by the time they got there. I visited the following day and what was once a lorry was now completely burnt out and had been towed to a lay-by. The cause could not be explained by Bernie or the fire brigade. The lorry was sold for scrap and Bernie continued in my employ for some time.

Later on a local solicitor, whom I knew well, asked me to speak on Bernie's behalf in a forthcoming magistrates' hearing. He was in difficulties with the law, having been accused of molesting a couple of young girls. He was a married man, with a lovely wife and children, and a very good worker, I decided to attend the court hearing and speak on his behalf. I was called and asked questions by the bench. I said that I found him to be a good and trustworthy worker. On summing up the magistrates emphasised that he was indeed fortunate in having a good employer to give such a reference. He was kept out of prison but bound over. During the following summer he decided to leave my employ at a minute's notice. About fifteen years later I was told by a friend that he had heard from a reliable source that the lorry fire was caused deliberately by Bernie.

I remember driving to Port Talbot to fetch a load of basic slag fertiliser. I had to wait in a queue of approximately forty to fifty lorries. I didn't get loaded for several hours and consequently it was late in the day before I could leave. Keen to get home back that night, I was driving hard and making good progress. There were no motorways in those days, the M5 didn't exist, and it was all A roads through towns and villages. To my horror approaching Okehampton on the A30 the brakes failed. There was nothing I could do except hope and pray for the best. I knew that if I could hold the road for approximately half a mile then the road would climb and the lorry would come to a halt. It seemed like eternity before the lorry came to a standstill with no mishaps. It was now late and with darkness having fallen, and not too much traffic around, I decided to carry on towards home, driving the next thirty odd miles on the gears only. Not an experience to be repeated.

The general haulage business and the hay and straw dealing was an additional source of income. We would go as far afield as Cambridgeshire, Hertfordshire, Wiltshire and Dorset to buy ricks of hay and straw to deliver to farms and markets in the West Country. It also had its failures. George, one of my drivers, not being fully acquainted with stacking a safe load of anything up to three hundred bales, was travelling along the main A4 near Newbury when he upset his load of straw and caused chaos. It happened on a rather sharp bend in the road, a high load and a certain amount of adverse camber meant only one thing - Off came the load and the A4 was blocked. Fortunately there were no accidents.

On another occasion it was a case of a lorry or maybe I should say a bus breakdown Brian my trusted driver and right-hand man had the bright idea of buying a cheap old bus and converting it to a lorry for hauling hay and straw. This was done and Brian went to Wiltshire to pick up a load of straw. Returning home through a small market town somewhere in Wiltshire the rear of the lorry partly collapsed, the tail part dragging on the ground. Police were called and another lorry had to be sent to transfer the load. Brian's converted bus did not have a long life.

On another occasion I took a load of Christmas trees to Spitalfields Market. I arrived in London at 5pm right in the middle of the rush hour, not knowing my way and driving a lorry fully loaded with Christmas trees. I found myself in Oxford Street making towards Piccadilly Circus. Following the directions given to me previously, I eventually got to my destination but it was closed until early the following morning. So to pass the evening I decided to try out some nightlife in the West End. I went to a club and once inside amongst the dim lighting with music playing, it being relatively still early I was targeted by all the attractive young hostesses in their scanty clothing. 'Are you here alone sir, would you like some company?' I paid for a girl to sit with me and entertain me for a short while. Of course they offered me packets of cigarettes, fifty in a pack which obviously I didn't want but if you had one cigarette you paid for fifty, and the same with a bottle of Scotch, if you had one little drop of Scotch you bought the bottle, and this was too expensive for me. So making some excuse I discreetly got out of this situation, as I walked out I said to the people at the entrance, as an excuse, I would probably be back later because a friend of mine I had been looking for wasn't in there. They accepted this story or at least I thought they had. I walked out into the dark alley and two men, one each side and just a little behind followed me. I kept my head straight and kept walking. I didn't know what the idea was until I realised they were probably two bouncers from the club checking up to see that I wasn't meeting one of the girls from the club. Anyhow I got into a well-lit street, they disappeared and that was one experience of London nightlife I didn't care to repeat.

The morning came after sleeping in the cab, the trees were unloaded and the business settled. I now had to find my way out of London again starting with getting through the narrow alleyways and busy barrow boys around Spitalfields Market. At least it was early morning and following instructions given by the market attendants I eventually got to the A1 without too much difficulty, making for Chatteris in Cambridgeshire to pick up a load of potatoes for the West Country. Not having had any sleep the previous night, driving to Cambridgeshire, loading potatoes and driving to Cornwall was a very risky business.

MARGARET

It was about 1969 and there were considerable business and domestic pressures. My wife Margaret had been ill and she was now home from Bodmin mental health hospital but she occasionally had relapses and needed to return for further treatment and rest. I was farming about 400 acres with an off-farm of 80 acres at Condolden, near Tintagel; there was agricultural contracting and the hay and straw business. I was employing about ten men, I was nearly fifty and I needed some assistance to manage these various enterprises. New legislation was imposed on lorries and haulage firms had to invest and update their lorries. Around this time I met Arthur Jory. He was about my age, soft-spoken, a devout Methodist and quite well known in the area. He was reasonably well liked but he was a failed farmer. For whatever reason that I did not know he had fallen on hard times and had to sell up. Arthur Jory was prepared to help me out of my difficulties and I smelt nothing but suspected everything not with hindsight the best way to start a business relationship. He invested some of his money and took over the running of the haulage and agricultural contracting. I was at this time quite involved with the contract spreading of slag, lime and sand on farms as far away as 30-40 miles and this passed to his day-to-day management. I was wary and cautious from the start and over time I was proved right. He was not to be trusted. I don't believe the arrangement lasted any longer than six months. It came to a showdown over some possible fraud on a cheque that was misrepresented or something. A meeting was called at my bank manager's office with Jory and my accountant in attendance. Jory was not aware my accountant Mr Hodgson of Launceston was also attending but he soon found out the seriousness of the meeting. His position was untenable and he was out and on my terms, put to him by Hodgson, he had to pay me the outstanding money for my share of the lorries. This was done and although my confidence had been knocked I had learnt a valuable lesson. Manage only what you can manage yourself.

Seven years after my first wife left me as already mentioned I married again in April 1955 to Margaret Smith at Launceston Registry Office. I vowed if I remarried, no mother in-law, no father in-law, and no money to interfere. I was 35 and Margaret was nine years younger with an unhappy background; father murdered by mother, she wiped the shotgun clean and made her daughter then twelve years of age, imprint her fingerprints on the gun as evidence. In writing this book I had to research the death of John Smith, Margaret's dad. Quite recently I called at Altarnun churchyard and could find no headstone of his so I went to Truro Records Office and dug out the burial records of Altarnun Church. I found without too much difficulty the record of John Smith as follows:

Number 698. Verdict at Coroner's Inquest: Accidentally shot by daughter, age 12. Abode: Trelawney Farm, Altarnun. Buried: 21 September 1941. Age 56 years. Vicar: William Kneebone.

Having returned from the records office with the dates and years, I went to the local newspaper office and they advised me to go to the library for the local paper's report on John Smith's death. (see below) I also called into Plymouth library to obtain copies of my enticement action.

During our courtship she told me what actually happened at that time. It was a difficult and very traumatic experience for her. It appears that John Smith was sitting at the table having his breakfast and Millicent, his wife, shot him at close range with the 12-bore shotgun in the back of the head. Death I understand was instantaneous. She wiped the gun with an oily rag to remove her fingerprints and immediately got her twelve year old daughter to hold the gun and thereby imprint her fingerprints on the gun as evidence. It was wartime, the local policeman did call and questioned Margaret alone for a few minutes stating "Did you have an accident with the gun my dear" This frightened little girl said yes. Nothing ever happened, the local bobby probably knew what had really happened. What she must have endured during the years ahead, being sworn to secrecy, not telling anyone, by the withholding of the truth. Bertha, her sister, has spent a large part of her time in a mental hospital. It certainly had an effect on Margaret's life and her future which did indirectly affect our relationship. She went through hell and through no fault of her own. It was an act of evil and wickedness done by a mother on her own daughter.

I realised early on in the marriage that I was the father figure plus the husband, and the total obsession she had for me was very real, but can one live with pity. I sometimes believe that I have had to carry a lot of the consequences of this murderous deed. Murder the most evil of crimes has its consequences on possibly several generations. My wife had been damaged by this in ways she or I or all the psychiatrists cannot fully understand. I do know that the crime went unpunished and undiscovered and I feel that the consequences of this act nearly sixty years ago were played out in my life and it was I am sure part of the reason for Margaret's inability to cope at times which was to cause difficulties time and time again throughout our long marriage. Margaret had five brothers and one sister and I noticed when courting her that there was not much communication between them. In fact there has hardly been any contact between her and her brothers and sister. Margaret turned against her mother after the age of twelve and her mother died in her own bed of old age back in 1970. Millicent was a hard businesswoman who dealt in cattle, ponies and farms. In my opinion not suited at all to having children. She did not greatly encourage her children to attend school, especially her daughters who were expected to wait upon brothers and uncles. Millicent farmed Trelawey and then Tredaule Manor at Altarnun on the edge of Bodmin Moor. Her husband John could be best described as being a bit of a rogue and brute. He had a reputation for being a hard moorland man, a good horseman who kept a racehorse but he was prone to a black temper, occasional hard drinking and a reputation as a bit of a womaniser. Margaret told me that she remembers her father hitting her mother and their volatile, violent marriage was subject to periods of separation. She also told me of an occasion when her father rode into Trelawney with a cow and calf in tow bought at market saying that they were a gift for his daughters and then he turned and rode off leaving his gift behind.

I first met Margaret when she was 23 and working as a live - in receptionist at the White Hart Hotel, Launceston. I would often drink in the White Hart on market day with my friends. I courted her for approximately three years, being very happy during that time.

We went to Scotland and the Lake District for our honeymoon in the spring of 1955. It was not an easy life in those days, but we were happy together and our marriage was blessed with four lovely healthy children; two boys and two girls. Money was in short supply and I was spending money in improving the farm's water supply, installing electricity, building large pre-cast concrete wide span sheds, removing a lot of hedges and generally trying to make life easier by mechanising and improving the farm. In 1959 I had bought Trenannick farm and bungalow. Managing the labour force was another problem. I had about a dozen men working for me in the early 60's and they all had to paid each week. The machinery used on the farm was also contracted out to work on other farms to make the machinery pay for itself and to keep the men earning their wages and me some much needed profits from agricultural contracting. I was, during these years, dealing in hay and straw, going to the counties of Wiltshire, Dorset, Hampshire and Cambridgeshire where hay and straw could be bought cheap off the field at harvest, brought down to the west country and sold at a profit to other farmers.

In the first few years of the marriage I was milking a herd of Ayrshire's and also keeping single suckler cows for rearing beef plus keeping about 300 pigs and a large flock of sheep. All this kept me very much on my toes, I was young, ambitious and had a young family to support. Looking back, I do now realize that my farm and business commitments had put a strain on the marriage. There was only one way for me to go to survive and that was forward. Margaret did her very best under sometime difficult circumstances looking after four small children, all being properly fed and clothed and sent at this stage to our local primary school. She had some help from either farm workers wives or sometimes we had a live-in home help. We had a relatively happy marriage for approximately the first ten years.

I noticed at times that she was very much possessed with me, she started to develop continuous headaches and migraines and often had to retire to bed for the day. The trauma of what had happened to her all those years ago was possibly at a much later date beginning to come out. She had had to live with this for many years and she was now in her early thirties when our marriage started to fall apart. Her health had deteriorated to such an extent that it brought about a major change in our relationship and in the lives of our four children

Margaret almost succeeded in April 1966 of committing suicide by taking an overdose. She was saved and recovered but was subsequently admitted into the mental hospital at St Lawrence's Bodmin for aftercare and treatment. I was lambing approximately 400 to 500 ewes indoors and in the thick of spring lambing. One late evening, approximately midnight, I was obliged to take a ewe with a lambing difficulty to the vet at Launceston, approximately twelve miles away. Before going I needed to change into some cleaner clothes, Margaret was already in bed and the two daughters were with her in bed. All still awake. Everything was fine when I left and I quickly drove to the vet's at Launceston.

Returning at about two o'clock, very tired, I unloaded the ewe and newborn, settled them in a pen and looked over the flock for any further problems. I was ready for bed. By this time the two girls were back in their own beds. Trevor was ten, Richard eight, Bridget six and Jillian a small baby. It was not long before I was sound asleep. Margaret was already sound asleep.

The following morning I was up very early about six and was careful not to wake my wife and I made an early inspection of the flock. Because Margaret had not got out of bed I was obliged to get the children fed and ready for school, driving them the two miles. Upon my return I went to the bedroom and tried to awake her but no response. I shook her and generally tried to wake her up. Just then I noticed the doctor's sleeping tablet container was empty and a paracetamol container was also empty. They were on her side of the bed on the bedside table. I hadn't noticed them before. I immediately phoned the doctor who asked me to again try waking her, with no results. He arrived shortly afterwards, phoned the ambulance and she was rushed to Freedom Fields hospital. I followed in the car with a police escort to the Plymouth hospital. There was not much the doctor could do because of the time factor. She was a strong person, she survived, but she did not regain consciousness for many hours, I think it was the following morning. At her bedside upon recovery she told me she was disappointed not to have done it. It appears that she had taken the tablets just as I walked into the bedroom to change into my clothes to go to Launceston with the sheep. Also she said that Bridget just aged six had said to her, 'That's right, Mummy take the tablets as the doctor ordered.' After her recovery and further medication she was transferred to the Bodmin Psychological Unit for a long time until she was deemed recovered and responsible. I visited her regularly, sometimes taking her out, on the odd occasion with the children. She continued having regular medication for her nerves and she periodically had to spend time as an in-patient at Bodmin Mental Health Clinic. Her sister Bertha had also been admitted to Bodmin at various times for treatment for her nerves but with her it was not because of a failed suicide. Margaret had to undergo electric shock treatment which gave complete loss of memory for a time. It is not easy for me to write about these things that happened to her. It put a considerable strain on me and our children, but I thank God that I was given the strength to carry on. Some years later I wondered how I managed to carry on through all this but I realise that there must have been a power that guided me through those years.

It would at this time be appropriate to mention that there was the very real fear of all our children being taken away from us and put into the charge of Social Services. What saved the situation was a lot of painstaking research and good friends, people who knew of my predicament and who helped by supporting me and possibly telling Social Services that I was capable of overcoming these difficulties myself. Trevor and Richard were sent off to St Petrocs a boarding prep school at Bude and Bridget was also sent to Fosters Melliers, a private school, also at Bude. I believe Bridget suffered a lot at the age of six of being uprooted and put into a boarding school. That was quite a traumatic event for her and I believe it has had longer term effect. Trevor and Richard seemed to enjoy their change of school and although Trevor could only stay at St Petrocs for just over a year, he did cry when I had to take him out of that school aged eleven and send him to the boarding annexe of the local state school at Launceston College. I did get a government grant from Social Services to help with the education but it was a great struggle financially to make up the difference and as soon as Trevor and Richard were eleven and old enough to enter the boarding school at Launceston college that is where they had to go. I could not afford private education for three children.

The three eldest were all away and in private school within a month of my wife attempting suicide and part of the weaning procedure that these schools used was that on becoming a new boarder the children were not allowed home for the first half of term. I had to wait two weeks before I could see them and I was only allowed Sunday outings to begin with. St Petrocs would have a regular Sunday morning school service at St Michael's Church, Bude, overlooking Summerleaze beach and the pupils used to walk to church in their school uniforms with shorts and caps across the dunes and the beach for the mile walk from their school.

It was after church on the Sunday that I was allowed to pick them up for the day, no visit back home was allowed for the first half term so also collecting Bridget from her school I would take them out for the day. The trip back from some local sight seeing, involved a visit to the usual Bude sweet shop to stock up on tuck. Sweets or tuck were rationed at the school and their Sunday evening purchases had to last them the next two weeks until I could see them again. There were at times plenty of tears from them on parting at the school doors. I would then drive to the cliff tops and downs at Widemouth Bay and sit in the car looking out over the Atlantic and shed a tear or two. After a while I found that bringing the children back on a Sunday to the farm every two weeks from school was too traumatic for all of us and we would go out for a Sunday drive and try to enjoy a visit to some place or other. Clovelly was a frequent place to visit. Margaret was away in Bodmin hospital for a long time and I tried to hold on to Jillian, but found after a time with all the farm work to do that she was not getting the attention she needed from me, although Shirley Aldridge the wife of my foreman was exceptionally helpful and Jean Edwards also helped out (she used to work for us in earlier years).

At the time I had a horse called Red Vale who incidentally had won a big race at the Cheltenham March Festival the previous year. The horse was in training with Tommy Jarvis from Kingsbridge. He, coming to the farm one day, said to me that his daughter-in-law would take Jillian from my hands for a while. He saw the position I was in and had sympathy for me and Jill. However I was reluctant to let her go as that was all the family taken (remember my enticement when I lost my wife and daughter) that was suddenly brought back to reality the second time around. But after a few weeks and a few near misses with Jill's non-attention, I decided to let her go to Mrs Doreen Jarvis and

Michael, her husband and their two children under four, who were about the same age as Jill who was fifteen months. On the day I was to take Jill to them at their farm bungalow near Kingsbridge I called in at Launceston with Jill in my arms to do some shopping so that I could present her in suitable clothes, getting near to Kingsbridge I decided to stop the car and do the necessary nappy change in a roadside gateway. Not being very professional in this line I made the best of it, and proceeded to the Jarvis's home, a bungalow connected to the farm where Mr and Mrs Tommy Jarvis, Michael's father and mother, lived. On arrival I was met by Doreen and her family and went into the bungalow with Jill, a very pleasant home with a special room for the children, with lots of toys and teddy bears etc. Jill was reluctant to let me out of her sight for some considerable time; she would leave me to just have a look at the toys but within a few moments was back in my lap. However, after a very long time she became convinced that I was not leaving her and she became more settled with Doreen and her young children.

Eventually I decided to go to the farmhouse where I stayed the night. During the evening I called to see her having a rollicking time in the bath and later as a peaceful baby fast asleep. I felt upset knowing full well that in the morning we would part. In the morning Doreen came with Jill in her arms to say goodbye. They were going to the beach for the day and to see Doreen's mum. I could not hold back my tears and became quite emotional. Doreen said that I could take her back with me. 'No, no, I cannot cope with it all.' Anyway they went on their way and after I left the Jarvis's house I had tears in my eyes until I arrived at the farm. No wife, no children, a dead unit. 'Pull yourself out of it', I said to myself, they are being cared for and educated, all having good health except Margaret and she hopefully would make a full recovery and things would soon get back to normal. 'Get stuck in with plenty of work to do, animals to look after, crops to attend to.' It was good therapy for me, not allowing myself time to feel sorry for myself.

There were the occasional times when I could arrange to pick up the children from school and take them to visit Jill at the Jarvis's. We would arrange to meet at Paignton Zoo and as soon as Jill saw me she came running with her small legs and came into my arms, and with what pleasure! She enjoyed the company of her sister and brothers but how short time is. In parting I put my children in the miniature train and Doreen took Jillian out of my arms and left immediately.
On another occasion I picked Margaret up from hospital for an outing to the races at Devon Exeter. Tommy Jarvis had a horse of mine running that day. How nice, I thought, Margaret could be with me in the paddock whilst the horse is being walked around and we could possibly have a photo taken to go with it. However it was not satisfactory and it all came to nothing and she couldn't remember a thing about it. We went to Plymouth before the races that day to buy a new outfit for her but she did not remember anything about that either, and when she later saw this outfit in the wardrobe she was suspicious of me having another woman. The treatment she was having was quite drastic, electric shock treatment to the nervous system, which can cause temporary memory loss.

However over a period of a few years she slowly improved and in due course she became more normal. However at times she did not keep up the medication prescribed to her, slowly and gradually she would get worse and she would have to be re-admitted to the clinic at later dates.

I am not sure, but Jill was at the Jarvis's home for approximately one and a half years. When she was there she became seriously ill with a severe and dangerous infection of enteritis. She was admitted to the Isolation Hospital in North Prospect Plymouth, somehow she had picked up some sort of a bug, developed a serious bout of enteritis and not being able to take in any food and she was also rejecting the drip feed. This alarmed the doctors who were quite concerned. When visiting the children could only look through from an outside window. I was allowed to go in but she was so ill she would not respond to any affection. The doctor and I discussed her welfare at length; he proposed that if Doreen decided not to take her back she could be fostered elsewhere. This I did not agree with, either I give her to Doreen for say four to five years and not interfere or I take her back with me to the farm. Upon her recovery, Doreen being unsure what was best for all decided on the moment that she would not take her back, so when I called at the hospital and saw Doreen's car with her clothes and toys etc, I knew that I was going to have my Jill back with me. I was naturally overjoyed and it was a wonderful feeling for me to take her back home. I arranged for Shirley Aldridge the wife of one of my lorry driver's to come in to help with the housework and also to help look after Jill who was now two and a half. She was such a wonderful baby and did not demand much attention, being quite independent and self-motivated. Within a few weeks of Jill's return Margaret came home from hospital and it had been a considerable time that there had been no contact between mother and child. Watching the situation very carefully I soon became aware that 'blood was thicker than water' and was pleasantly surprised how they quickly reformed the bond of mother and child.

DRUGS and HIPPIES

MARGARET never much liked living in the farmhouse, she felt it was too remote and wanted to live in the farm bungalow at Trenannick a distance of one mile. The bungalow adjoined a quiet country road so there was hardly much improvement in closer contact with the outside world. I suppose because of her sickness and all the children except Jillian being away at boarding school, I went along with the idea and even welcomed the move. I thought it would be practical to let the farmhouse and earn some extra money.

How or where I advertised that I had a remote Cornish country farmhouse to rent I cannot remember but I did receive a response from a young couple, I believe they probably came from London or possibly from overseas. Tony was tall, well-built, aged early twenties. He seemed to be well educated and I thought a suitable tenant. His girlfriend was of similar age, rather attractive, short, blue eyes and long shoulder-length auburn hair. She had an American accent and showed me a reference from a professor at Yale University. I decided they were suitable and, having asked for the rent, which was paid in cash, there did not appear to be any problems. I did not take up or obtain further references and in my naivety I did not even give them a tenancy agreement. The American girl loved her cats and a few of them came with her. Cats, if trained, are very clean, however these were quite the opposite. The smell and the state that the house was left in when it was eventually vacated was beyond anyone's imagination. Music appeared to be their living and pleasure, and there was a lot of coming and going by various people, some staying for a short time, and some staying in the farmhouse for longer periods. Some were guitarists and associated with bands. I remember one winter night they gave an impromptu band rehearsal at full amplification in the old piggery. My two teenage sons were rather impressed at having a live rock band playing at midnight and into the early hours. The noise could be heard for miles and this caused quite a stir from the locals and quite a bit of curiosity as to what was going on at Fentrigan. The tenants, Tony and his girlfriend would often be away for long periods (I later gathered, abroad). While they were away others came and stayed. I suppose it was treated by their friends as some sort of Cornish backwoods hippie commune; an attractive young blonde girl was a regular visitor who eventually stayed along with others. With the farm as her last known address her father, an army colonel, concerned as to his daughter's whereabouts, notified the police, who made a visit to the farm.

It was just a routine inquiry about a young girl who had not been in contact with her parents but what followed was anything but routine. The colonel's daughter was not at home she had had a severe attack of asthma and was admitted to the local hospital for overnight treatment. A friend of hers or Tony's with his wife and child stayed at the farmhouse that night. Having driven a long way they took advantage of a night's rest before intending to move on again in the morning. However at about 10am there was a knock at the door, it was the police and without waiting to hear what they wanted the fellow made a run for it, out the back door and up across the meadows. The single policeman gave chase, caught him and asked for reinforcements. This was suspicious, why had this guy made a run for it when they only wanted to ask about a missing person? Drugs were immediately suspected. Then all hell broke loose. The drug squad with their sniffer dogs turned the whole place, over farm buildings and fields included.

It was spring and I was busy lambing. It was very strange to have a lot of well-dressed police officers looking around my lambing shed in the midst of slimy newborn lambs and bleating ewes. I was in my dirty clothes, unshaven and looking unkempt and quite annoyed at their intrusion and even more annoyed when a mare and new-born foal were galloping excitedly around the meadow because a police sniffer dog was searching hedgerows. They eventually found, later that morning, what they were looking for, seven kilos of cannabis resin hidden in the seat linings of a car. The Chief Constable of Devon and Cornwall was brought in, there was press interest as well.

Seven kilos was quite a catch and the Fentrigan Farm drug bust made the lead television news story on the News at Ten that evening. They arrested several, the man; his wife and child were taken off by the police who took possession of the house awaiting any further visitors who happened to call. As callers came they were taken away for questioning. It was early one morning, very dark and windy, when the tenant Tony returned to the farmhouse alone. On entering the unlit house he was immediately accosted by the police. Frightened, he realised he was a possible accessory to the whole affair. I saw very little of the tenant, apparently he and his girl travelled frequently to the USA, Canada and other countries, returning to make brief rare visits to the farm. When we did meet he always appeared to be in a hell of a hurry, having just arrived, wanting to be off again abroad. His girlfriend would at times go with him. She was arrested with him and both were on their way to Exeter prison on remand awaiting trial. At the eleventh hour he raised bail for both of them by getting a cable to confirm he owned a valuable music manuscript in the safe keeping of a New York bank vault. She eventually jumped bail and fled to her home in the US. Tony was taken to court for this and was sentenced either to prison or had a hefty fine to pay.

This was the first big drug bust in Cornwall and it certainly made headlines for me as well. I was not in any way involved and the local papers gave quite favourable reports regarding my character. I also had to take a lot of stick and leg pulling from friends and colleagues. Tony called on me a number of years later. He was found innocent of any charges relating to the drugs bust and he told me how he was guitarist to a Japanese rock group who owned a jet aircraft and flew around the world giving concerts. While in Morocco he had a car accident and had an operation on his leg, leaving one shorter than the other. It was the colonel's daughter who made arrangements to fly him out of Morocco to the United States where he was operated on again to fix his legs satisfactorily.

LAMBING and SHEEPDOGS

I HAD known Sidney Cobbledick for many years. Sid had a smallholding near Tresmeer a few miles and ten minutes by tractor from Fentrigan. He was married with children. Living in a rather ramshackle place, the yard littered with old tractor bodies, various farm machinery implements and general junk. He was a local lad making an honest living by offering his services to farmers. He could do everything from shearing to combine harvesting. He often used his own equipment charging by the hour and could turn his hand to any work connected with farming, he was very capable. He was an extremely good-hearted, hard working, honest man who would help anyone who was in need.

He had a large stomach and a rocking gait, a full round face with a beard, somewhat weatherbeaten by exposure, standing nearly six feet and of a sturdy build and nature, dressed always in heavy type working clothes normally covered in oil or manure or both. One only saw Sid in a suit only at funerals and other such social occasions. He had a unique loud raucous laugh, throwing out his stomach and body and laughing 'Yah ! Yah ! Yah !' usually in threes. His normal greeting to me was: 'Hell's bells, how be 'ee today?' Sometimes he entered the house and gave a rundown of local news. He recently died, quite suddenly whilst sitting on a tractor, it was possibly heart failure. He was very popular with all the local farmers.

I had a lot of respect and admiration for him: there was a time when I was obliged to ask Sid to step in and take over the indoor lambing of approximately 500 ewes. I originally intended to handle the lambing season of about six weeks by myself without any assistance, however after about a fortnight working around the clock I became quite shattered and was going around like a zombie.

Before bringing ewes indoors for lambing, we lambed outdoors. During heavy frosts the lambs would be born and frozen to the ground. In bad weather conditions they would die at birth or after a few days. Foxes were another hazard, taking the lambs immediately on birth. Also I had a mad sow which, having taken a lamb from its mother and eaten it, went chasing around the field with its nose in the air sniffing out for more lambs to eat. When a pig tastes blood it can become quite violent. I recall a sow having her litter of pigs and as soon as a pig was born she would get up immediately and snatch it up to eat. This went on until she polished off the whole litter.

Lambing before we had a lambing shed was a difficult and painstaking operation, especially at night, when they would choose to drop them. When the weather was wet sheep would present the lambs at a faster rate than when the weather was dry and cold. If a ewe should lose its lamb, one skinned the dead lamb and put the skin on a live lamb and hoped that the ewe would accept the foster lamb. If not we would confine the ewe to the stocks until she accepted, but not always. When housing ewes in large numbers sometimes a ewe would take away a newborn lamb from another ewe before they had their own lambs, often more than one lamb would be taken. The big problem then was to find the lamb's real mother. That made it essential for someone to be on the site at all times.

Sheep are very sensitive to the smell of their new born lamb and it soon becomes imprinted upon them and is their ultimate form of recognition besides the recognition of the bleating of ewe and lamb.

Difficult births were sometimes a problem with me. I happen to have very large hands. When Sidney took over he was exceptionally good at taking lambs off at birth. It became obvious that lambing about 500 ewes, each ewe producing approximately two lambs, and trying to save as many lambs as possible meant some support was needed, especially the time consuming work of looking after the weak, and to bottle feed and attend to these weaker lambs would save large numbers of lives. Farmer's wives or female lambing helpers are very good at giving this delicate and nurturing type support at lambing time. Lambs were sometimes put into a warm lower oven in the Aga or beside an open fire to revive them from the cold. I have revived lambs when they have been nearly dead by putting them into a hot bath, but there is the risk of their dying later of pneumonia.

For me, without assistance and a patient assistant (man or woman) the losses could be very large. However I did try for a fortnight but in the end Sidney was called and he took over completely and I have to accept that he was a professional at lambing ewes. I returned to my bed and left him in full charge until lambing was completed. On a good lambing season we would end up with about 160-170 live lambs per 100 ewes put to the tup, these mostly going to the fat market or abattoir during the summer. In autumn the barren ewes were culled, the old ones were sold off and younger ewes were reared for replacements.

I went to Wales with a friend many years since and bought a lorry load of two tooth Cluns. A few years after, I decided to have a flock of mule bred sheep, very prolific with good mothering qualities and reasonably docile. I went to Appleby market in Carlisle and bought hogs (one year old sheep) with their lambs during May, approximately 300 hogs with lambs, one large three-tier lorryload. I stayed at a local hotel and the following morning watched the system of selling in which sheep were taken to a ringside, walked around and sold in fairly large numbers.
One had to be very guarded because if it was known that you had travelled far and bought a pen of sheep, they knew you would have to purchase a lot more to make up the load. However prior arrangement with the auctioneer and the haulier covered that potential hazard. I was also rewarded with the system known as 'luck money'. Buying a pen of sheep, the haulier went to the farmer who was selling, and collected a percentage of the sale in cash for him, and came to the rostrum with the money for me. At first I did not understand, but I soon gathered sufficient knowledge of the local custom of 'luck money'. This money paid all my expenses and those of a long-lost female friend, who accompanied me.
This trip and subsequent annual trips proved successful. I also went into the Welsh borders and into Wales and bought a pedigree Texel ram for 900 guineas. I did have

some problems lambing my young ewes because the Texel breed has a large shoulder with a short neck and this caused problems, especially lambing the younger ewes. The breed however was popular with butchers and housewives, having a very lean carcase.

With a large number of sheep, especially the Welsh hill breeds, the fences had to be good but with hindsight my fences were not up to scratch. A lorry load of small Welsh hill ewes was delivered one night at midnight, the lorry was large and could not get into the farmyard to unload these fast hill roaming sheep and put them into a field. I found out later that they were self motivated with minds of their own, taking off over large distances. After a few weeks of hassle from neighbouring farmers fed up with my trespassing Welsh sheep I decided enough was enough, gathered together what could be found of the flock and sold them on to a farmer with wider pastures.

A good dog is very necessary with flocks of sheep. I have had a few very good border collies and one appreciates an intelligent dog, equivalent in value to a man. These dogs however had quite a problem to get ahead of the Welsh breed, when really motoring with heads down, tails out straight it was a race as to who would win. Normally when one has worked dogs with sheep the collie breed know the move the sheep intend to make and cover it. There have been many occasions, driving sheep and cattle on the road, when the dog goes over the hedge to get in front of the animals, goes to the crossroads and guides them through to the road you intend to travel.

One day in the farm drive I was surprised to see an Alsatian dog and a crossbred sheepdog attacking a lamb and eating it whilst still alive. This was quite unusual, and my sole object was to try to get the dogs, get their confidence and eventually put them into the car boot. I kept cool, took hold of the less aggressive sheepdog and tied him with some coloured twine to the car. Handling the Alsatian was not so easy, however with a few pulls at the lamb I eventually succeeded in getting the dogs into the boot of the car. I called the police and we called at a neighbour who denied his dog was involved until, hearing his owner's voice, the dog barked and he recognised the bark. He accepted it was his Alsatian, telling us he had been with them for several years and was a quiet, sensible dog. He agreed to have the dog put down (his wife became very upset) and no further charges would be brought against him. We never found the owner of the sheepdog, which was put down. I called a vet to have the lamb destroyed

One of my earliest collies was Ben. I had Ben for several years. On one occasion I was returning from Hallworthy Cattle Market with a large number of unsold cattle. They got too far ahead of me and my collie dog Ben took off in pursuit but owing to the narrow roads and the crossroads ahead, I thought the dog had also lost touch with the cattle. Having waited for at least half to three quarters of an hour near the farm entrance, to my surprise I saw these cattle were being brought back with the dog following behind.

One of my young bullocks strayed onto a neighbour's field and got mixed up with his cattle. Ben and I tried to part them to bring my animal to the farm. This proved impossible as my bullock would not leave the company of the others. I was about to give up and started to walk away and leave Ben to it, but he persisted in trying to separate my bullock from the others and in time his persistence paid off. Eventually trailing the single animal all the way home we brought it back to the farm.

Ben was in the habit of running out in the road when a car was passing. He was hit by a vehicle and left lying at the roadside. I was away that day and was told the following morning by telephone what had happened by the local person who had run over the dog. The dog had been left as dead and put by the hedge. A little later to my surprise the dog, covered with hoar frost, arrived at the door. I took him indoors by the fire and then to the vet. He said there were no broken bones but there could be brain damage, gave him an injection and warmed him with hot water bottles. One marvelled that Ben was still alive. After a long week or two he very slowly began to improve, staggering and wandering for several weeks after the vet's visit. We were obliged to keep him indoors. If he had been allowed to go free he would have wandered off and got lost which happened on a few occasions. At one time he travelled four to five miles to another farm. On searching we eventually found her and the family was reunited and very happy to have Ben back. After approximately six months he was showing progress and eventually recovered.

Our neighbour from their own line of good working collies gave me a puppy, which to begin with I called 'Puppy'. I never did get around to giving her a name and we both soon became so familiar with the name 'Puppy' that is the name this most loyal and intelligent dog was to receive. She probably deserved a better name but she was with me for several years. The name 'Puppy' probably suited her; she was most playful and inventive. We had a few free-range hens; Puppy would get them together and put them in their chicken pen at night. She was especially good at handling sheep, rather timid with cattle however, she did very little barking unless the animal concerned proved to be awkward. With a large flock of sheep she would keep them together by weaving in and around and, if one or more tried to stray, she would soon get them back in the fold. I was amazed how she would handle a flock at a considerable distance manoeuvring the sheep either individually or in numbers, silently and effortlessly and sometimes out of my sight.

We also had a few ducks. They were rather aggressive and took control of the farmyard. It was quite amusing to watch them strolling with a flutter of their wings, with a lot of 'quack quacking', dictating their terms to Puppy. She usually took the easy option of moving away.

I did not attempt to take Puppy away from the farm when eventually, at the age of sixty-five, I moved out of the farmhouse to let my younger son Richard take over with his wife Gillian and their two year old son Nicholas. I had by this time started living and doing some property development in Plymouth where my eldest son Trevor and his wife Sandra were living. Trevor had started buying and converting older large properties into flats. He started with converting one house into three flats after graduating from Plymouth Polytechnic and it developed from there. I followed his lead and started doing the same in Plymouth, often working together with him on various projects, sometimes on my own, using my own sub-contractors or on one or two occasions employing my son's building company on some of the larger projects.

I was away from the farm for quite long periods while living in Plymouth and moving my lifestyle away from farming. On returning to the farm I was always given a rapturous greeting by Puppy. Before I had a chance to get out of the car she would be there, paws up against the car door looking longingly at me with those eyes of hers and once her head was resting on my knee, I could hear her saying: 'Where have you been old friend? I have missed you! You have let me down.' She would then become quite excited and would run around the farmyard in that way dogs do when very happy.

It became evident after a while that Puppy was becoming quite deaf, possibly caused by an incident a few years earlier. She had been chasing one of the horses in the meadow and had got kicked in the head. I was there at the time it happened, it sounded as though a gun had gone off, she was taken to the vet and seemed to make a full recovery although she had quite a long spell convalescing before she was back to her old self, but with more respect for horse's hooves.

Puppy was also in the habit, as are so many farm dogs, of chasing tractors and running in front of them trying to bite the revolving wheels. This was to be her downfall. As time wore on her deafness became very bad and being, as well, slower through old age, she was not as quick in her reactions and was run over and killed by one of the tractors. I was away at the time but I still feel some sadness when I go to the farm and she is no longer there to greet me.

Two Jack Russell terrier puppies, called Whisky and Spotty, both dogs from the same litter were bought by me as pets for the children. Being terriers they were full of spirit and character and were a lot of fun for the children but they did love to chase things. Anything would do but unfortunately they chose sheep. They were not of an aggressive nature but one day not long after leaving cute puppiness behind them they both decided to chase some sheep, I was with them at the time but unable to stop them. One sheep broke away from the flock; the dogs continued to bark and harass the ewe that was exhausted and frightened. Driving the Land Rover to them they were still barking at the frightened sheep, I decided to go for them in no uncertain way and give them a good hiding. Spotty the larger one fearing what was to come, jumped into the rear of the Land Rover, whimpering and shaking. Both he and his little brother got the hiding they deserved and after this there were no further problems. Spotty was run over and killed a few years later by a car but Whisky lived to a good old age becoming a close companion to Jillian, my youngest daughter.

One summer afternoon in very hot weather, about seventy Friesian two year old cattle, pestered by flies and the heat, broke out from the field into the road one mile from our local village Warbstow. A large number of cattle will easily break into a run with the excitement of a strange environment and the noise of their galloping hooves spurred them on and eventually into a full blown stampede. It was impossible for me and my favourite collie Fly to get ahead of them. The road was narrow with high hedges, and such a large number of stampeding cattle presented great danger. Walkers, cyclists or anyone walking with a baby in a pram would most probably have been killed.

As they stampeded toward the village a building site seemed to divert their attention and the leading animals decided to charge through the new housing estate, crashing down fences, barriers and gardens until they met a bank with approximately an eight feet drop into a farm lane. Charging down over the steep bank into the lane they ran on for a further half mile until finally coming to a halt at a farmyard. It took quite a while for them to settle before being returned to the paddock.

HOUSE on FIRE

IT WAS the summer of 1976, the year of the great drought. It was August and it had not rained for three months, streams on the farm had dried up and only the main spring at the back of the farmyard was still running. I have never known this spring ever to run dry in nearly eighty years, indeed the name Fentrigan is derived from the old English word fenter which means spring. This spring water is collected as it trickles from the bedrock in the side of a hill. From the collection tank it is pumped to the farm reservoir at the top of the farm in the highest field about four hundred yards away and from there feeds by gravity to the farmhouse, farm buildings and the drinking troughs in some of the fields

We had been running the farming partnership for approximately eighteen months and there was a lot of stock to be watered. There were a hundred and fifty cattle, which had to have water carried to drinking troughs in the fields by tractor and some large improvised water tankers.

On one of the hot August days, when I was away at Hatherleigh market buying sheep, that Richard and Trevor cleared out the attic of an old wagon shed. They burned the rubbish safely enough and then loaded a trailer with firewood and scrap timber collected from the attic. The load was taken to the bungalow which we were then living in and unloaded against the end gable wall. There was, however, a disaster waiting to happen. Unknown to the boys they had unloaded one piece of wood which must have been still smouldering from the earlier bonfire they had held at the farm. It cannot be known for certain but some ten hours later at about midnight this piece of wood was probably responsible for the woodpile against the gable wall catching fire.

 It was all tinder dry and in no time at all the gable end hip roof of the bungalow was well alight. The whole bungalow was destroyed and burned out before the fire brigade could arrive. Imagine my shock at arriving home close to midnight to find our house ablaze. After the market I had visited some friends at Holsworthy, staying till late and on driving home I noticed when still a few miles from home a glow in the night sky. When I reached the top of the hill about a mile away I was horrified to see the bungalow in flames. What went through my mind were the worst of thoughts, it must be the worst fear of any husband and father to return home late at night to find his home on fire. Fortunately all the family were outside and safe.

It was not long before the police and fire brigade arrived but there was nothing more they could do other than douse the remaining flames of an already burned-down dwelling. Three engines came; Camelford, Launceston and Holsworthy, but the bungalow was already well ablaze before the 999 call was made. Trevor had made the call, he was at home watching late night TV, Margaret and Jillian were asleep in bed and Richard and Bridget were out. Neighbours returning home from the pub at about 11.30pm were driving up the back lane and observed across the small field that the bungalow roof was well on fire. Trevor was in the lounge but had not heard anything untoward, but he did hear the telephone ring in the hall and went to answer it only to be told by our neighbours that the house was on fire. He then heard the blaze in the roof, got his mother and sister awoken and out of the house and called the fire brigade. It was very fortunate that the neighbours telephoned and raised the alarm. Jillian said that she had not been feeling very well that night and was actually in bed with Margaret instead of in her own bedroom at the far end. She and Margaret were fast asleep and were awoken just in time as the ceiling was already falling in and flames in the roof space above. If Jillian had been in her bedroom it might have been too late for her safe escape. The house burnt down in a matter of minutes. The only possessions Trevor managed to save were the family photo albums kept in the lounge. Everything else was lost including some ancient family documents, and we were left with what we stood up in.

My sister Sylvia who lives nearby put us up that night and we were fortunate that we could soon move back to the empty farmhouse at Fentrigan. I was missing my loyal sheep dog Fly for some time after the fire, Trevor and others told me that she was definitely outside the bungalow during the blaze but this was before I had arrived home. A few days after the fire I decided to start to clean up the and under the burnt-out bed lay my dog Fly. I was very upset at this, I thought he had survived the fire and had gone missing for a few days through shock or fright. To find him burned to death under his master's bed was more than I could take and I broke down into uncontrollable tears. He had evidently gone into the burning house that night thinking that his master was there in his bed and loyal as he was he wanted to be with his master at the end. Trevor and Richard buried him for me in the garden.

Within a year the bungalow was rebuilt, most of the walls were sound but at £3,000 it was considerably underinsured. In 1978 we moved back in as Margaret preferred living in the roadside bungalow rather than in the farmhouse at the end of a half mile lane. For a while her mental health improved, I believe the shock of the fire and the loss and of having to recover from such a situation made her pull herself together. This brief recovery lasted for about a year but she inevitably returned to having me and nothing but me as the centre of her universe.

I found the marriage very difficult at times; she had an obsessive love for me and still does. This was and could be destructive at times to any happiness between us. An example of this was a short holiday we had, a weekend away about a year after the fire, I believe it was 1977. Trevor and Richard had organised this as a surprise weekend trip to Longchamps, Paris to see the Prix de l'Arc de Triomphe. It was the first time that Margaret or I had ever travelled overseas but I did not enjoy it as she created a scene by making herself drowsy and ill by taking too many tablets and she destroyed any sense of enjoyment of the racing or of our first taste of foreign travel.

HORSES: BREEDING and RACING

FOR several years I didn't have any horses on the farm, I had had enough of them as a young man, I really welcomed the machine age which took away a lot of the tiresome drudgery of working with horses. As soon as I started farming on my own accord and when farming with my brother at St Mabyn we were glad not to see another horse. Mechanisation had arrived and not a moment too soon as far as I was concerned. Of course there now exists in the younger generation a romantic, nostalgic attachment to working with horses on the land. There is no romanticism on my part; I only remember too well the reality of it all! Work, work and more work with slow inefficient horsepower.

I must have been about forty when I began to take an interest again in horses. This time the interest was kindled by family connections. Margaret's brothers Charlie and Wesley Smith were keen amateur point to point riders and had a few racehorses of their own which they had bred themselves. I began to take an interest and I soon had my first half share in a racehorse. Jointly owned with Wesley with him doing the training and race riding at local point to points. I began again an involvement with horses after a lapse of almost twenty years. This time of course it was racehorses and for leisure. I never really had a hobby; I didn't play golf or sail or have holidays or any of those leisure interests. I was a busy working farmer with 400 acres and a young family of four children and this 'Sport of Kings' was to be my leisure, pleasure and grief for almost the next twenty years.

In those twenty years of racing I experienced both the lowest of lows and the highest of highs. From having Jill's Pet (named after my daughter) destroyed at Wincanton races to standing as a winning owner in the winners enclosure at the Cheltenham Festival. I never made any money from racing but it gave me a lot of happiness and lifelong wonderful friends. I was very appreciative of that aspect. Farmers especially in my locality can be insular and introspective. Having racehorses was my escape from the insularity and isolation that I felt as a farmer.

'Jill's Pet' was a bay mare, standing at sixteen two hands, a thoroughbred aged five years. I did have some difficulty with this horse when breaking and riding her. I decided to go to the local hunt for a day's sport. You had to attend with your horse to at least three hunt meetings of the local hunt you were registered with to qualify the horse for the point-to-point meetings and National Hunt meetings. The day in question, having been saddled and prepared for the hunt, she began to sweat and became very excited. I eventually got on her back and she seemed to become uncontrolled and the sweat was running off her as through a hosepipe was turned on. I stuck with her, galloped for a few miles, hoping that she would settle. I stopped for a breather; she reared up on her hind legs and pawed with her front legs. I was sitting on a horse that was standing on her hind legs. About to go over, I gave the reins a tug and she rolled back over, missing me by inches. Friends of mine witnessed this experience. I presume the horse had a brainstorm of sorts. After some weeks I decided to send her to the trainer, Martin Pipe of Cullompton. Eventually she was entered to run at Wincanton in a novice race. The trainer was most impressed with how she was responding and gave me some confidence in the potential of the horse.

The jockey took hold and they looked a good combination as they rode in front of the stands prior to the race. Once around the racetrack and on the second run around, as it was a flat course, one could only see the jockey's head rising and falling at the far end. I was standing with the trainer by the stands when the horses completed the race except 'Jill's Pet. We walked around to see what had happened, getting nearer to the fence we heard the sound of a gun. My first reaction was to turn away but I followed through and saw my horse dead, blood from the forehead and a broken front leg. That was my worst experience in racing. The best experience was when Red Vale a twelve year old giant of a horse standing seventeen two hands who I jointly owned with my brother in law Wesley won the prestigious Foxhunter Chase over four miles at the March Cheltenham Festival. On recollecting I think the year was 1964, Red Vale was ridden by a Somerset farmer and point to point rider George Small. At halfway at one of the large fences he unbalanced and temporarily lost his reins. Recovering, he won the race, I think there were twenty odd horses in the race and nearly thirty five fences. He was at 14-1. I did put on a tenner to win; also the prize money was around £8,000 with a cup. The excitement was terrific. Bertie Piper from Chillaton, the trainer, could not speak for some considerable time, being overcome. This was a Westcountry horse and I was involved later with celebrations at the Chillaton Arms, the cup being filled and refilled with a strong beverage keeping everyone present in good spirits. Later I sent the horse to Tommy Jarvis near Kingsbridge. He entered the horse at Ascot, Sandown and a few Westcountry races but did not win again. The horse, when retired, was put into a riding stable near Hatherleigh. He eventually died having an ulcerated stomach. When the horse was at home at Fentrigan, Trevor my eldest son, aged nine years, would ride him out around the local lanes. Red Vale was of a very docile nature the horse would not hurt a fly. Trevor was quite a small boy and, the horse being over seventeen hands, it was like a mouse sitting on an elephant.

Moonarise 1970 (Middle)

I had another racehorse called Sunarise, which I jointly owned with my brother in-law Charlie Smith. I had bought from Charlie the brood mare Chiltern Hills or it may have been Cotswold Cottage from which he had bred Sunarise and I subsequently bred a half brother with the highly original name of Moonarise.

Now Moonarise, when a few years old needed to be gelded, and George Sutherland the Launceston vet who knew a fair bit about racehorses and the racing world came out to the farm one fine summer's day to do the castration. Firstly Moonarise, being halter broken was taken into the large empty hay barn with plenty of clean straw strewn around and then George proceeded to give him an injection of the tranquilliser with the dosage calculated according to bodyweight. We waited for ages, no effect, none at all, another injection, the horse staggered a bit, but still not sufficient. George said to me 'What is this you've got here? The thorough thoroughbred?' and he gave him another jab, and that put him to sleep. Then he did the incision on the scrotum, removed the testicles, put in the biodegradable stitches and that was that, all over in a few minutes. A few hours later Moonarise awoke, stumbled and staggered a little while overcoming the tranquilliser and he was possibly none the wiser that he went to sleep as a colt and awoke as a gelding. Whilst waiting for the horse to recover George told me of the dangers of his profession and that some years ago a young West Country vet trying to inject a horse with the anaesthetic slipped the needle and instead of going into the horse it went into his body and he died within seconds. Lethal stuff.

I did own and run over fences and point to points some other horses called Bossinney, Sabeechi, Dunheved and Cornish Princess, but no winners. I bred these and a few other horses from my brood mares, putting and covering them with thoroughbred HI (Hunter Improvement) stallions at various studs in the West Country. When Trevor was twenty he worked at David Barons racing stables near Kingsbridge in South Devon. It was only for a period of six months and though he could ride reasonably well he was keen to try point to point riding in the forthcoming season. He moved into lodgings with a neighbouring farmer near the stables on his twentieth birthday in December 1975 and I delivered him there together with two five year old horses to the racing yard. The deal with Baron's was that Trevor would work for no wages but get to ride out and gain experience and work in the yard and I would get both Sabeechi and Bossinney into training with a well known National Hunt Trainer. Sabbechi was to be entered in National Hunt hurdle races and Trevor would ride Bossinney in point to point races. Trevor enjoyed his time there, went to some National Hunt races as a travelling lad as far away as Uttoxeter, Warwick and Oswestry. He rode in three point to points that season without any success at being placed but in his last race at the Morwenstow course he was coming to the last fence in third place but sadly he was unseated at this last fence. When he came back to the farm after the six months was up the horses came back too. These two horses were later sold, as we no longer had the time to put into training them at home and they were unlikely ever to prove to be racing winners.

It was at this time in the summer of 1976, the summer of the great drought, on Trevor's return from his spell working in a racing yard that we decided to form a farming partnership of W H Grigg and Sons. Trevor was twenty, Richard eighteen and myself fifty-six. I was in some respects proud to be forming a partnership with my two young sons but in other respects it was an ill-thought-out decision. My instincts said no but love for my children and the optimism that all business owners have of hoping to be able to pass on the baton to their offspring was too strong in me. Margaret and I were happily married for a long time in the early years of marriage and for the past ten years we have been legally separated. When we left the farm in about 1984, Margaret and I rented a house at Plympton a suburb of Plymouth. The owner was going to America for a long time and the plan that I had was to carry on with property conversions in Plymouth using my son's building company and my own team of tradesmen. I did not want to use my scarce amount of capital (as the farm was still heavily in debt from the failed partnership) to buy a house for Margaret and I but to buy more properties to convert. I was determined to clear most of the debt on the farm overdraft and the only way to do that was to earn some pretty good profits from property conversion. I did not wish to divorce her, but a once and for all settlement was eventually reached, giving Margaret two flats in Citadel Road on Plymouth Hoe, one for her to live in and a top floor flat which was tenanted. She could collect the rent or when the flat became vacant she could sell the flat. The only property I now owned was a dilapidated terraced house in Baring Street, Plymouth awaiting conversion into two flats and I continued to live on my own in rented accommodation. She had filed for a separation order and it was granted in 1988.

THE FINAL YEARS

The year is 1997 and after approximately two years of indecision at last I have decided to follow on with my story and make it as complete as possible. Recently my medical condition has deteriorated, I had a hernia operation in 1995, then heart problems in the autumn of last year when I was in Derriford Hospital, Plymouth for two weeks, making very slow progress against a deteriorating heart condition, and then prostate problems. I have prostate cancer, which was diagnosed this year at a stage where containment by drugs is possible but there is a chance that the cancer will spread. A scan has identified bone cancer which according to the experts can be contained. Hence a final effort to put pen to paper and try to finish my story. Despite my limited knowledge of writing I either decide to go ahead or throw in the towel and write nothing more. I need to continue.

I have always made it clear to my children that nothing is more important in life than the enjoyment of good health and happiness. I have had my share of disappointments and some of those were through possibly myself having differing expectations of my children than what they had for themselves. Children grow up to be adults, to lead their own lives and I believe I have tried and succeeded in allowing this. I have always been there for them but they have to make their own mistakes and learn from them, they are adults now with their own families and they know that they can always come to me with their difficulties if they wish. I am proud of each and every one of them, I have nine grandchildren and I hope my children pass onto theirs the values that I have tried to instil of honesty, hard work and the Christian value of doing unto others as you would wish to be done unto yourself.

I met my partner Carole, at a party given by Trevor, my son in January 1990. Trevor was living on his own in a rented farmhouse near Yealmpton and was recently separated from his wife. He had invited several of his friends and of course I was invited along with his brother and sisters. Carole and I soon became very close. She is thirty years younger than me and I sometimes tease her as to what she finds attractive in me. It's not as if I can leave her anything. I've already given everything away and I had lost money on a barn conversion that I built at Holbeton, a village in the South Hams. I had hoped to have been able to live there in retirement with Carole but the building society eventually repossessed it and we ended up moving back into Carole's house in Peverell, Plymouth. She has nursed me during my recent illnesses and has been a wonderful companion and source of comfort, strength and inspiration to me through these past eight years. If it had not been for Carole I would probably have already been in my grave and she also instigated and encouraged my renewed contact with my long lost daughter Janet. Getting to know Janet has been a wonderful experience for both father and daughter and I have at this late hour been attempting to do whatever I can to allow Janet to get to know the father she never had. It was through no fault of mine that she was taken from me but I am grateful to Carole for having helped to bring us back together.

It is spring now. The year 1998 and I am 77 years of age with a varied life behind me, I have written a factual story of events in my life and I trust interesting to the reader. No doubt he or she will make their own observations. The best summing up of this book and of all that has happened to me can be no better put than the words of my late father which were told to me by a family relative at my father's funeral. She told me of the time when she saw me as a little boy waiting for a train with my Dad at Otterham Station. She said to him 'What a bonny boy you have there, Richard.' My dad's reply was typical of him: 'It's a good job that he doesn't know what's in front of him.'
I think that about sums it all up !!

Me aged 74

72nd Birthday Party

Fun with the children & grandchildren

Lewis & Sam (1990)

Katie (3) 1995

James (4 months) Easter 1998

Kate Christening

Trevor age 4

Richard & Bridget

Trevor at Torquay

Trevor at the Royal Shakespeare Theatre

PART THREE
– A STORY OF MY TRAVELS –
CANADA

It was 1984 when I took a touring holiday in Canada with Thelma. I had met Thelma through some farming friends at St Tudy near Bodmin in about 1978. My only previous experience of foreign travel was an unenjoyable weekend away in Paris the previous year (1977) with Margaret. Thelma was recently divorced and she was decorating some holiday apartments for a friend when we first met. In due course a few months later we became close friends and although I was still living with Margaret; firstly at the farm and later in Plymouth I did enjoy seeing and meeting with Thelma on fairly infrequent occasions. We had both been through very difficult times with our respective partners and we decided in secret from all members of both our families to get away from it all and take a holiday in Canada. We flew from Gatwick to Ontario hired an automatic car and went firstly to Niagara Falls and took a trip by 'Maid of Mist' to the base of the falls. We were provided with waterproof clothing. The roar of the water and the spray and mist was quite something to remember. We stayed a few days at Niagara and then moved on towards Lake Ontario. Near Ontario we saw huge grain silos where lorries and trains deliver grain and then ships are loaded from these huge silos. I was allowed to have a look at the workings by taking a lift up to the top. We visited a large agricultural show which was well below the standards of an equivalent show back home. Passing by on a Sunday morning a church service in a certain farming region, we noted all the churchgoers dressed in black with their ponies and buggies, approximately a hundred of them tied up outside the church during the service. These farmers have no television, radio, festivities, no tractors, being excommunicated from the sect if they break their laws. We also visited a very large farm, with several hundred fat Herefords being fed on hay silage, a pedigree herd of Simmentel bulls and Charolais bulls with their own annual private treaty sale which was attended by buyers from all over the world. The farm manager drove us around in his large truck and told us the owner was a German businessman.

From Ontario we hired a car and drove several hundred miles further westward until we caught the Canadian Pacific railway and took the train all the way across the huge expanse of the Canadian Plains and the Rockies to Vancouver. From there we took a flight back to London. This three weeks had been a wonderful experience and I wanted more. At the age of 64 this had been my first real taste of foreign travel. It was a further two years until I was to travel again. I continued to see Thelma on our return from Canada and she had bought her own basement flat in Plymouth and was beginning to get her life sorted after a protracted divorce. It was to prove short lived. Thelma died in 1986 of cancer.

MORE TRAVELS – CHINA

In the autumn of 1986 I went on a package holiday with about thirty other adventure minded tourists to China. The package was not for the faint hearted as it involved a very busy itinerary over 28 days and we were warned of course that some of the accommodation and travel arrangements would be very different to what we may have been used to. The China trip proved to be most fascinating and I enjoyed every moment of it. What follows are some of the experiences I had of this most fascinating country and it's people.

Visiting a township we saw real poverty, and the floors were of earth. The cooking was done by an open fire in the corner of the room. The Chinese pigs were within the home compound just next door from the living quarters adjoining the cess pit where the excreta from the humans was disposed of in a shallow pit covered by a galvanised sheet. On occasions the sewerage from the cesspit was collected by a man with a bicycle and a covered trailer towed behind, which was taken some distance and spread in the field for fertilising the crops. The water was drawn by a winch from a communal well. The roofs of their homes were of galvanised metal sheets and secured down by stones and rocks. The roads were full of holes and very muddy. Seeing this was enough but to see the poor, sparsely clad small children looking at us, so helpless but seeming to be pleasant enough, I did feel for them and, having a few sweets gave them to the children. They at first did not respond to me but after I ate one myself they took a few. Our courier noticed what I had done; he did not approve. Apparently it is not the normal procedure to hand out gifts to anyone unless they earn it in some way or another. It may encourage them to beg or even steal in later years. This was told to me quite forcibly.

At a Chinese infants school we saw a display of dancing by the pupils. The teacher playing the piano and the small children from about five years of age doing a type of dance with to and from movements, arms under their chins and combining their style with suitable fast movement, this varied style changed from time to time. Children being well presented and showing their best behaviour. When the show ended we all gave a show of appreciation of their efforts by a show of hands. Taking their places behind the wooden desks and chairs and saying their goodbyes in Chinese, we left. On returning later these same children with their teacher were waiting by the roadside to wave us on our way. I thought that was a touching experience.

Having a full day ahead after staying at one of the community centres, which incidentally was not a pleasant experience, having the surprise visit of a friendly rat in our room, also the smell of the mosquito deterrent in the form of a burning lamp, lying on a hard wooden bed protected by a mosquito net and sparsely covered. These mosquitoes were very active and one could hear the familiar buzz, buzzing, hoping that they would go away. Having taken Chinese tea and a little food, which was prepared in the communal kitchen area of the farm, we made our way to visit some rice paddocks. The area in which we were accommodated was a small part of the township. A township consists of approximately 25,000-30,000 people, all being completely self-supporting in education and hospitals, producing their own food. When and if there is any surplus food that the township does not require the producer can, with the permission of the local chieftain, sell the surplus in the local market place and with the money he can buy a few necessities for his home. It was understood that this was not a popular scheme with the authorities, as having a better standard of living brought discontent to the local inhabitants.

Having left the communal kitchen we boarded our air-conditioned coach and we visited an area of wheat and rice production. The water was raised by a method used in biblical days, by standing on a wooden treading contraption and as your weight moved the step along and you had to keep up the pace. The water would be brought to the surface and channelled along to the man-made channels to various routes to water large areas of rice and wheat. As an alternative to man using his energy to pump water to the crops they used a water buffalo tied in such a way that he could not but keep going around in circles, having a type of harness attached to a wooden beam and an attendant with a whip to keep him going around and pumping the water. This I found quite fascinating, especially having a try at the man-made contraption, when I found it quite hard to keep up the pace. Apparently two people usually work the system.

We drove along the road, noticing that the peasants were cutting the wheat with a hand sickle, bringing it to the roadside and laying it out on the road. I could hardly believe my eyes. Lorries, coaches and cars were hardly seen and all the lorries and coaches were government property. However the ever resourceful Chinese peasant would lay the wheat on the road so that it could be partly threshed by the passing wheels and the peasants would come along afterwards with their brushes and pans to collect the grain. Further along on the route road making was in progress; men and women by the hundred and very few machines were seen. Women were breaking stones and carrying loads of earth on their backs with a yoke and two wicker baskets. It was like watching ants at work. The coach stopped for a short time for us to watch this phenomena. They would gather earth and stones from a very large pit near the road and then running up the man-made hill, tipping the earth and stones, first one basket then the other, and then running down to the bottom of the quarry and repeating what must have been a monotonous and laborious labour.

Bicycles were evident everywhere frequently with small trailers being towed loaded with everything imaginable. Mules were also used to pull loads of stone, bricks and other very heavy materials; these trailers were made of wood and put together in a way that it amazed me to see that it withstood the test of time. The long mule trailers with their wooden tyres when loaded were almost dragging along the road. I stopped at one point and went to stroke one of a pair of mules, as is usual for me, being involved with horses. Getting close, I was about to put out my hand out when suddenly I was faced with a violent surge towards me and a large open mouth showing a shining set of teeth at the ready. I made a hurried retreat to the amusement of the group I was with.

At one of our regular morning meetings prior to a farm visit we were invited to join the Chinese head and his staff for tea and a discussion on their farming methods and our programme for the day. This was done through our interpreter and the Chinese courier who stayed with us during the whole tour. Incidentally a fresh courier was introduced to the provinces that we visited, presumably being acquainted with and specially trained for that particular province. Tourists are restricted to particular provinces and regions or towns within a province. The authorities only wanted tourists to see what they could control. If one did wander off the route previously mapped out by the authorities there was the risk of being arrested. I also noticed that the hotels were situated somewhat out of town and manned by disciplined staff who must obviously have studied languages to qualify. They were of a high standard and well equipped. I noticed that television was available in some rooms, but not all hotels had them in the bedrooms. Programmes were very restricted, and vetted, with no sex, vice or violence shown on the screens. Your laundry was collected, cleaned, ironed, folded and presented back to your room in an immaculate condition. Guards stood at the hotel entrances, vetting all travellers and others connected with tourism etc, the reason being that the outside Chinese world did not know the standard of living that the westerner was accustomed to, hence keeping them at a distance and being so detached was the reason the authorities used such disciplinary measures. They used ingenious methods to repress the ordinary man in the street. You could not indulge in any type of work; you were regimented and controlled by authoritarian overlords who were situated at various points to control the working of a successful township. To qualify for Western tourism the township, over many years of hard and conscientious work, through strict discipline and at the discretion of the authorities, would qualify, not forgetting all the citizens working together like bees (all for one and one for all). Any lazy bees would not be welcome in the hive. Every township had a shop where various articles were made. Having called and begun to barter over some articles that I wanted to buy, I left and joined the coach for a short trip to see some paddy rice fields. Only then realising that I had left my camera on the counter of the shop, I was given permission to return to the shop to recover it. It was only a short distance and, having returned, I looked in the area where it was left and, not seeing the camera, word soon got around and I was astonished to see how everyone made such an effort to find it, to no avail. With time running out I returned to the waiting coach and was assured by the Chinese courier that I would get it back. He questioned me in depth to make sure that I had not made a mistake. I did have a witness to prove that I was in possession of the lost article. The camera was returned to the hotel the following morning intact. I was told that apparently everyone, men women and children were gathered together in that particular compound locked into a large hall, and one lost camera had to be accounted for. I also understood that it was the normal procedure that the culprit could lose his finger, ear, or even have his hand cut off. Again if it had not been found in that compound it would have had to be reported to the Chief of the township. He was responsible for any serious misdeeds and could take any appropriate action he thought fit. One also realises that to get the privilege of having Western tourists to visit their township, in the past the citizens had to put all their effort into setting a high standard for the authorities to qualify and pass this township for the tourist industry. The losing of a camera, however simple, could jeopardise their future tourist status and other townships would have gained by their loss.

As I mentioned earlier every township is completely self-supporting. We saw a hospital, which seemed more like a gathering of cripples all sitting or lying with acupuncture needles stuck into different parts of their bodies. Seeing the misshapen legs and arms one wonders what these people must have suffered during their early days.

We saw a duck rearing enterprise, literally thousands of them, traffic was halted for a while so that they could be guided across the road to a very large lake and enjoy a swim before feeding time.

Being shown the largest silk factory in China was an inspiration. At first we were taken to see the mulberry trees and leaves and the silkworms and then a factory tour. The noise that the hundreds of looms were making was simply unbelievable; you could not hear your own voice if you shouted. The very young and some elderly people were working by the hundred at these premises, not wearing any ear protection. The decibel rate, being extremely high, will leave them deaf in a short time. These looms were imported to China from the UK at a give-away price, as we no longer had any use for them in this country. Further along the line we saw hundreds of rolls of silk of various colours being stored ready for the market.

Early on in our tour we had a journey by coach from Beijing to the Great Wall of China. It's not only great; it is 'enormous'. The wall dominates the skyline as it snakes its way for thousands of miles. It is quite an experience to climb along the almost vertical points at places and eventually arrive at one of the many lookout towers. It's the longest structure ever built by man, 1,500 miles long, and constructed over 2000 years ago, intended to keep the people from the steppes of Asia out of the rich heartland of China. We also visited the Ming tombs, burial site of thirteen of the Ming dynasty emperors. The road to the site is lined with huge animal sculptures, lions, elephants, camels etc. Later on we visited a number of tombs of different dynasties.

While in Beijing walking in Tiananmen Square, the largest in the world, our party visited the Temple of Heaven, a masterpiece of geometric 15th century architecture, and the majestic Summer Palace, seeing also Chairman Mao's body lying peacefully, being guarded by soldiers situated at each corner. The people were all dressed in traditional 'Mao' style clothes and with their caps looked terribly drab. Chinese people would stop and stare, would follow us and would if possible come so close as to touch our western style clothes. This was quite embarrassing until we understood their motives. One of our group, a lady, had prominent ginger hair and caused quite a lot of interest to the Chinese. We also visited the Forbidden City and this massive area with the Imperial Palace and a host of other temples of past dynasties, too numerous to mention, which were, as the name depicts, forbidden to all except the emperors, empresses and their concubines and slaves etc until recent years. They are now available to the general public.

During the evening we enjoyed a Peking Duck Banquet at a large restaurant. One thing that did strike me was the smell that came to meet me as I entered the entrance to the toilet. Having enjoyed the meal, and departing from the restaurant, I was met outside by a Chinese man offering us a ride in his rickshaw, a light two-wheeled hooded vehicle. A large Yorkshire farmer and myself alighted and sat there for a little time. In a very short time a very large number of Chinese had gathered around, being curious as to why we were getting so much attention other members of our group started taking snapshots of us and the group. The crowd of onlookers was now so large that we were losing sight of our party. Eventually the rickshaw started to move off with his two passengers on board. Pedalling down a sharp, short hill and going away towards where I was not quite sure, we left the couriers in a dilemma. Our spontaneous impulse to move away and detach ourselves from the group we realised later was a ludicrous thing to do. However the couriers quickly got the rest of the party back on to the waiting coach and eventually found us, to our relief, at a coach station about one mile away. We were questioned at length, almost interrogated by our Chinese couriers. One of them was so exasperated by our naive, undisciplined and adolescent attitude. In his view our actions were so incomprehensible that he gave us a good lecture and dressing down.

The following day we flew from Beijing to Xian, visiting the Terracotta Warriors. This great historical discovery in 1974 by peasants digging an irrigation well unearthed thousands of life-size terracotta figures guarding the main entrance of Qin Shi Huangdi. It is estimated that six thousand figures are buried at the site, which also contains horses and golden chariots. At the site a very large hall has been constructed to view the warriors. Xian has 8,000 years of history and was at one time the largest city in the world, and was the capital of China under eleven dynasties. It was a major trading link with Asia and Europe. In the afternoon we visited a small-scale farm commune system.

The following day we flew from Xian to Nanjing. During the afternoon a coach took us on a tour including the Yangtze river bridge.

The following morning we took the train from Nanjing to Wuxi, we were served with the traditional green tea, which I did not particularly enjoy, however I did enjoy relaxing and looking at leisure at the passing rural scenery. The train was not very fast and the ride provided an ideal viewing platform; to see their farming methods and how they improved matters by their own adaptations and ingenuity. I could not help but feel despondent on their behalf and with an element of hostility toward the authorities for using as I saw it slave labour to survive. The peasants were not in any way allowed to progress on their own initiatives but to work only for the state and on a very meagre living wage. One also realises that if the Chinese, being a fifth of the world's population, were to be allowed to have our Western way or even a taste of it, they would soon have another revolution on their hands. It will take many years to transform China, if at all. They need considerable infrastructure such as roads, railways etc, and also the economy would not stand up to the pressure of so many people wanting improvements. Shortly after my visit there was the serious rioting and the subsequent crushing of the revolt in Tiananmen Square. I can understand why. One of our couriers was a girl student and showed me around one evening part of the university, which she shared with another girl student. She was well versed in politics, spoke good English, hence her part time work as a courier. She could not leave China for another country unless to pursue a high standard of education with the ultimate purpose of such education to be utilised for the furtherance of Chairman Mao's philosophy. Sometimes one had the feeling that you were being watched and scrutinised.

Having explored Wuxi we took a leisurely cruise on Lake Tai, one of China's largest lakes, and visited a clay figure workshop and an acupuncture school. After a visit to Wachi Village Brigade known for its very high productivity, spending lunch with them and studying the progress of the agricultural output by the commune, the following morning we boarded a canal boat for a leisurely cruise to Hangzhou on the picturesque West lake. We saw gardens, temples and tea houses which makes Hangzhou typically 'Chinese'. On arriving at Hangzhou we were guests of the farming faculty at Hangzhou University, which I found very fascinating. Afterwards we visited another commune whose major crop is the well known renowned Longjing Tea (Dragon Well Tea), which is harvested three times a year and processed with great care to preserve the quality and the flavour. We took a further cruise on the West Lake and relaxed before driving south of the Yangtze River to visit a farm in the Shaozing area, spending the day meeting farm managers and workers, which I found very interesting indeed.

AUSTRALIA & NEW ZEALAND

1988, I was sixty eight years of age and I decided to go and visit my youngest daughter Jillian and her boyfriend who were spending a year in Australia and New Zealand. I had good friends out there in Australia too. Jill was staying for a while with her godmother Jane and her husband Leo. Several years ago Jane had come to live at Fentrigan in the annexe with her two very young daughters Helen and Sandy. Jane took a job as a home help for Margaret after her return from hospital and she also did some work with the horses. Jane was divorced and was down on her luck but she worked hard, never complained and was determined to rebuild her life for herself and her two young daughters. She eventually met and married Leo and for a while they took on and ran the pub at Mary Tavy near Tavistock. After a few years of this they sold up and emigrated to New Zealand and after a few years there they moved to Brisbane and have been there in the same place ever since. I decided to travel out there to see them and meet up with my daughter and her boyfriend Michael. I had kept in touch with Jane and Leo by post over the years and they were really pleased I was coming out.

1 September 1988

I had flown from Heathrow the day before and I had a one night stopover in Singapore. I left Singapore for Brisbane a day late as the flight had been delayed from the previous day. Received a free dinner and an extra one night at Grand Central Hotel till 4.00am rise to catch the flight. Jill and Michael met me at Brisbane airport and we drove to Jane and Leo's at Jimboomba.

2, 3 September 1988

Had a local look around the town, Jill took me to several travel agents for further information as I wanted to explore Australia and New Zealand

4 September 1988

Jane, Leo, Jill, Mike and myself went out for the day, I saw rain forests and hang gliders in the mountains.

5 September 1988

Jill took Michael to work and then we spent the day at a travel agent and got tickets for flights and hotels and three tours. Jill and I had a night walk in grounds expecting to see a wallaby but no such luck, only a frog.

6 September 1988

Preparing for leaving on my first tour tomorrow afternoon. I am going to Cairns. Jill goes to work picking strawberries. Invitation out this evening with Leo and friends.

7 September 1988

Leaving on an Air Australia domestic flight for Cairns, a two hour flight and checked in at 11.30am at the tour Hotel Acacia Court, 230A-238 Lake Street. By 1.30pm I was on the tour. Firstly we toured the city naval base, seeing the huge marinas and a huge bulk sugar terminal with acres and acres of sugar cane. Further inland I saw crocodiles being fed on a crocodile farm, snakes being handled and a replica of an opal mine.

8 September 1988

7.15am start with a one day tour of Cape Tribulation and Daintree involving a four wheel drive adventure. We started the tour with a large bus but after about fifteen miles the clutch packed in and we had to wait about an hour for some replacement four wheel drive Toyota station wagons holding about twelve each. The roads were terrible, large potholes, crossing crocodile infested rivers and I had my photo taken with one of the party standing in a stream with a backdrop of the largest fern in Australia. All the rain forest is very thick with all types of trees, white maple, mahogany and red cedar, some being approximately 600 years old. The fig tree is similar to our well known parasitic ivy but grows much bigger and can eventually strangle the tree. Also saw the stinging shrub whose sting can be with you for many months and also the black bean tree. Scientists have recently undertaken trials of the black bean and could have found a cure for AIDS from this tree. A lot of the world's medicines or their precursors come from the trees and shrubs of the rain forest. I saw Japanese tulip flowers growing on trees and a fig tree with figs shooting out from the timber. I saw the best tea in Australia being grown, the same tea shrub lasts for one hundred years and the leaves are periodically clipped from the bush. We heard of how the turtles had disappeared from Turtle Cove when the road work started. I saw wild pig in abundance and we also crossed a crocodile infested river by a fairly flimsy ferry. Crocodiles can stay under water for two hours, eat only two kilograms per day and can go without food for two months. One lady two years ago was dragged in from the ferry and never seen again. They store their prey in hidden areas and return in time to have their fill from the larder. I returned back to the hotel at 7.30 pm and organised a trip for tomorrow, the Barrier Reef. I may try snorkelling. Alarm set for 7.00am.

9 September 1998

I was booked on the Quicksilver a fast trimaran which at a speed of 27 knots got us to the Great Barrier Reef in one and a half-hours. I tried the snorkelling but I was not very good, instead I went by underwater boat to admire the fantastic colours and shapes of the reef. It was truly an amazing sight, fishes of all types and sizes. We spent the day on the reef returning in the evening. Over a pint I met the owner of the largest sail trimaran in the world.

10 September 1988

Took a trip by train and then coach to Atherton Tableland, very scenic indeed. Saw sugar cane farming land, a remote out of the way village and orchid gardens. The journey was on very winding roads through rain forests.

11 September 1988

Cancelled an all day trip on a canoe river ride. The previous evening I had met by chance some Cornish émigrés Bill Owen and his wife Penny. He took me flying in their two seater Cessna over Cairns, Greenstand and Michaelmas Stand reefs. Then he flew over the rain forest and followed the Barron George railway back to Cairns, very scenic. Lunch with their family and then a trip to some botanical gardens by a lake. We had a few drinks and then dinner at the airport club and they kindly returned me to my hotel at approximately 10pm.

12 September 1998
Went out shopping in the morning and bought a pair walking sandals and a video of Cairns. Got some photos developed and then caught the coach to the airport. Flew to Darwin on a three and half hour flight and checked into the Boulevard apartments.

13 September 1988
Left 6.30am for Katherine by coach on the Stuart Highway. Visited a war cemetery including the dead from the Japanese bombing of Darwin. Visited Pine Creek open cast Gold Mine and saw huge earth moving equipment in use. The gold seam runs underneath the highway and they are moving the road to get it. Went on a trip by boat in Katherine Gorge, very scenic. Lunch in a makeshift round shed erected by the coach driver and some inquisitive wallabies and emus approached. It was very hot and everything was scorched brown and the trees were stunted. Stayed that evening at the Pine Tree Motel. Had a good swim in the pool.

14 September 1988
Leaving motel at 8.00am for Never Never Country and Cutta Cutta limestone caves. Harmless snakes in the caves and saw stalactites and stalactites. Told that tights go down, mites grow up. Onto Mataranga, swam in a thermal pool with palm trees around. An oasis in a desert. Lunch, then called at an aboriginal settlement, saw buffalo and wild pigs. Also saw a few kangaroos in the wild, exotic birds and thousands of termite nests. Rains can be very heavy when the season permits, the creeks were now dry but impassable when the rains come. We returned the 250 miles to Darwin via Stuart Highway through Mataranka, Katherine, Pine Creek and Adelaide River. There was very little farming in this northern area of Australia

15 September 1988
Took a bus trip and sightseeing of Darwin Museum, Jannine Bay Gaol and the military museum. Saw the damage done by Cyclone Tracy on Christmas Eve 1974. Went to a large market in the evening and later visited a new very large modern casino and hotel.

16 September 1988
Early departure leaving 6.30am for a trip to Kakadu Park, drove on the Arnhem Highway and Adelaide River through wild country. Took a boat trip at the Kakadu holiday village, everything was very plentiful with dangerous crocodiles nesting in the water and banks, numerous birds of all types and saw buffalo. Lunch on board the boat which was tied up to the shore. Afterward to Obiri Rock. Many paintings on the rock by aborigines, some thousands of years old. Returned to Darwin 7 pm.

17 September 1988
I had been making my own way and as soon as I arrived somewhere I would sign up for some sightseeing trips and get to see and learn a lot about the place. My next stop was to be Alice Springs, and take off was at 2.40pm. I phoned for the airport bus for 1.40pm but it did not arrive and I got into a bit of a panic so I got a taxi and arrived just in time as the gate was closing for the Boeing 727 for Alice Springs. I found accommodation two kilometres out of town in an outback motel for the night. I joined a coach trip the following morning at 7 am for a two day trip to Ayres Rock.

18 September 1988
We passed a cattle station called the Mount Ebenger ranch of some 7,000 square miles, with thirty people working on it, three head of cattle per square mile and three helicopters. We passed a windmill and the next service station was 700 kilometres away. We were told of a Mr Lassiter who found gold in the 1800s, returned to base and after many months set out again to look for the rich gold seam. He never found it and perished. Many people have died trying to find the gold. It was in this region that John Flynn started the Flying Doctor service. We passed the Stanley Chasm and the MacDonald Ranges, one of the world's oldest mountain ranges. We passed riverbeds, now dry but in the rain season they become raging torrents. I had a photo taken of myself standing with Mount Olga in the background. Arrived the Ulara Hotel approximately 1.00pm and I left again at 2.30pm for an afternoon trip to view the Olga's and to see from there the distant Ayres Rock. I learnt something of the vegetation from the tour guide, the Ruby Dock has a red flower, the Pea Flower, Desert Oak, Pine Tree all apparently flourish and the sap of the Bloodwood shrub is good for sore throats. The Whitichi bush is very prevalent. The water to Alice Springs is supposed to come underground from New Guinea thousands of miles away. Ayres Rock we would visit tomorrow. It is the world's largest rock, 846 metres above sea level. The Rock itself is 348 metres high and 9.6kilometres in circumference. Near Ulara we saw a water hole and it is a place of ritual for aborigines. Twelve to fourteen year old boys are circumcised here, they are held down and also their breasts are cut across by sharp stones. Muda tree bark sap is rubbed in to stop the wounds from festering and then the boys are turned out into the bush for two to three months and have to survive. If they are timid and soft they usually die as no one of their tribe will acknowledge them. Any male aborigine with a scar on his chest signifies what tribe he belongs to. Also tribes have their sacred places where their women have their babies, under rocks in a squatting position. The aborigines only paint what they know and can see such as trees, animals, water. There are approximately 250,000 aborigines in Australia and they have been given back some of their land by the government, such as Ayres Rock area and other national parks which are very large and sometimes granted on long government leases.

Ayres Rock

19 September 1988
Left Ulara 6.30am for Ayres Rock, arrived 7 am. Started the long uphill climb, exactly one hour before reaching the top. Signed the book and started the descent, very scary at times but returned back to coach at 9.00 am. The sun was beginning to get unbearably hot as it was much cooler early in the morning. My legs felt rather rubbery. It was a 450 kilometre coach trip back to Alice Springs. I had an early night as it was another early start in the morning for another sightseeing trip.

20 September 1988
Left 8 am for a trip to Palm Valley. Went through the MacDonnell ranges, viewed Sleeping Dog mountain and Jay Creek. Visited an Aboriginal community and then out to Missionary Plains. The Owen Springs Station, Sydney Kidman's first property, a large meteorite crater and Mount Sander (Sleeping Lumbra). Arrived at Hermannsburg built by Lutherans who established a settlement in 1877 for the aboriginal population. There was an aboriginal funeral assembly in progress with much wailing and cutting of flesh. One man was bleeding quite heavily from his grief cuts. We then went down to the Finke River and it's gorges, it is the longest river in Australia but was dry at the time of my visit. When the rains come the water level rises to twenty feet or more above the dry riverbed. The gravel and sand road is the riverbed, and it was very rough terrain for many miles. When the road is flooded there is no access at all to this region The river flows and drains into huge salt lakes towards the southeast. Eventually we arrived at Palm Valley. The Livistona Marina is 200-300 years old. It used to be a tropical oasis in a desert. Stayed at the Palm Valley Chalet which was very primitive and basic. There were no toilets and the walls were made of a wood frame with a covering of leaves to keep out the sun. Visited the Cyad Fern Tree and also another sacred place where babies are born under the rocks. Then to Namatjira Memorial where we viewed Gosses Bluff meteorite crater. Albert Namatjira is a world famous aborigine painter and his paintings are worth thousands of pounds. Returned at 6 pm to hotel and had an early night in preparation for a mid morning flight to Perth.

21 September 1988
Arrived in Perth after a three hour flight from Alice Springs, had to set the watch back by one and a half hours. Saw the Olgas, the salt lakes, Lake Rason and Lake Carey etc, from the air. All 2,000 kilometre is literally barren. Arrived at the New Esplanade Hotel, Perth.

22 September 1988
Took a coach and boat tour to Freemantle, they had recently suffered the worst storms for thirty years, and it was the American Cup Yacht Race that year. Rolf Harris and film stars have houses in Millionaires Row in Swan River. I took a tram ride to see around the town of Freemantle and returned by boat to Perth and went to the Hilton Sheridan for an evening.

23 September 1988
Went to Perth Royal Show by train, I took a photo taken of a Merino ram worth 20,000 dollars. Met some interesting characters and saw all type breeds including a lot of English-bred cattle and sheep.

24 September 1988
Went on a boat trip to wine tasting, very good trip, well organised, good lunch in superb surroundings, free flowing wine.

25 September 1988
Day out with Arthur and Molly Berryman who were friends of Jane and Leo, picked me up from the hotel and took me on a trip into the country. They invited back to their place for lunch and I stayed till 6.00pm. Returned me to the hotel and we had a few drinks together. They left, I had a meal and met an interesting man and we talked a lot, mainly about farming.

26 September 1988
Early 4.30am start as I am flying at 6.00am to Adelaide. Now have to set the watch one and a half-hours forward. On arrival in Adelaide I posted a letter and a card, had a walk around and organised a trip for tomorrow. I had left my spectacles on the plane, I phoned Australian Airlines and they phoned back and told me that they had found them and they were at the airport for me. They kindly offered to forward them that day to my hotel. I would have been lost without my glasses.

27 September 1988
Stayed at Ambassadors Hotel in King William Street. Looked around the city by coach and also took a trip out to the vineyards in Barossa Valley and did some wine tasting. Lunched there and returned late afternoon. I had left my camera behind at the vineyard departure lounge.

28 September 1988
After two days moved on from Adelaide to Sydney. Stayed at Tudor Hotel, Kings Cross. Plenty of nightlife took two tours of the city by night and visited some clubs. Dinner and entertainment was Aussie style, a sheep was clipped on stage, and the food was served real western stump style. Took a trip on the overhead and underground rail system which is basically a two tier train system. Took a coach trip around the city, one dollar to go anywhere, train or bus. Went up to the Blue Mountains, very scenic, a 310,000 hectare park. Rode on the overhead cable car, passed the famous Rosehill race course, the Parramatta River and heard about Granny Smith apples. She threw them away in the mid 1800's some French crab apple seeds without knowing they were crossed by accident and grew wild in her garden to later become recognised as a world famous apple variety. Finished the tour on time and then the MacQuarrie inn, the oldest pub in Australia. Took a harbour boat to see Sydney Bridge which was imported in sections from England and also saw in the harbour one of the world's largest warships - the Ark Royal which had once been visited by us all back home at Plymouth Navy Days when she belonged to the Royal Navy. Visited the Opera House it was built in 1964 at a cost of the sale of lottery tickets paid for it. Some facts: seats 2,690 people, the outside is built from special Danish tiles, inside it is all wood, Australian wood, and the acoustics of this magnificent building are allegedly the best in the world. The huge organ cost $1,200,000, it has 10,500 pipes. After a long day I returned to the hotel. My camera had been returned to the Tudor Hotel - lucky me. Tried that evening to contact Van Copp the son of a good

friend Mervyn Copp from Launceston. Van had left for Amsterdam a few days before. I also got in touch with Leslie Hawkey who had emigrated from Cornwall several years ago but they were going away for a weekend.

1st October 1988 to 3rd October 1988
Spent two more days sight seeing in Sydney. Saw a huge flotilla of ships for commemorating some special occasion. Left Sydney for Brisbane by coach 7.15pm, arrived next day 11.00 am, very tired. Stopped for dinner and breakfast on the way. Went through Gosford, Newcastle on the Pacific Highway to Charlestown, Princetown, Taree, Langatta, Southport all along sixty miles of the Gold Coast and a surfers' paradise, it was very difficult to find accommodation and very expensive. Stayed at the town of Olims at the Kangaroo Point Motor Inn. Jane and Leo came at 5.00pm, stayed for dinner and saw the Expo fireworks from balcony. They left at 11.00 pm

3 October 1988
Early morning call at 5.30 to be at airport by 7.00am for the flight to Auckland. Rode downtown through Auckland by using the post office van which also doubles up as a bus service. Took me to my motel and I immediately phoned Helen. Helen was Jane's daughter, she was now a grown woman and married to Ian and the last time I had seen Helen was as a little thumb sucking five year old all those years ago at Fentrigan. My credit card had expired on the 30th September and I could not check in to the motel. Helen and her husband Ian picked me up and I stayed with them for a few days. I had been expecting a message at the airport from Jill but there was no message. Jill and Mike had moved on from Australia and were now planning to work their way around New Zealand.

4 October 1988
Phoned Richard regarding my replacement credit card which was at Fentrigan. I asked him to send it by courier express to Helen's address. Had a quiet day, met Mrs Tretheway (Senior) Helen's mother in-law

5 October 1988
Ian and Helen showed me the city of Auckland, saw the sights, the docks and the ships.

6 October 1988
Trip by coach to Bay of Islands to Piahia, stayed the night there, a very scenic drive on the way there.

7 October 1988
Trip to Bay of Islands by cruise boat, missed a day trip to Cape Reinga and a coach trip to the ninety mile beach. Instead took a cruise to some other islands and saw the Hole in the Rock but the sea was too rough to go through. Took a photo of the replica of Captain Scott's Enterprise. Some of the Islands are privately owned, in the early 1800s a manager killed all of a family who owned an island, he was tried and hung in Auckland. Called at a small town called Russell, which at one time was the capital of New Zealand. Left early afternoon by coach for Auckland and early evening I was met at the coach station by daughter Jill and Helen. Organised the car to tour the North Island starting tomorrow.

8 October 1988

Replacement credit card arrived in the morning post from home. Off by coach to see North Island and to pick up hire car. Sent birthday card and letter to Lewis.

9 October 1988

Jill, Mike and myself collected the car and set off to Thames. Drove through fantastic scenery, lakes, rolling hills, and forests. Drove on passing through Whangarnata, Waihi, Katikati, Tauranga, Okere Falls and then to Rotorua for the night.

10 October 1988

Trip to the Whakarewarewa thermal area and saw the huge geysers, 60-90 feet in height, bubbling mud and steam everywhere. We saw a Maori Arts & Crafts Institute. Drove through scenery, blue and green lakes, to Tarawera, the buried village (1887) by the eruption of the mountain Tarawera. Drove on to thermal area (Waimangu), very interesting, whole lakes boiling and bubbling, steam everywhere then on to Cathedral Rocks again huge clouds of steam. Saw a thermal power station in the final stages of construction. Stayed at Lake Taupo for the night.

11 October 1988

Left for Waitaki and saw the world's largest thermal power station which produces 5% of New Zealand's power which taps the steam from a bore approximately 1,800 feet deep. Travelled onto Huka falls, roaring mass of water viewed from bridge, approximately quarter of a mile in length. Stayed the night at Tongariro National Park to see the volcanoes but it was foggy so nothing was seen

12 October 1988

Returned to Pukawa, near southern part of Lake Taupo. Picked up coach at Turangi. Very scenic drive to Taihape. Did see the snowbound volcanoes this time. Saw rolling hills, very green and thousands of sheep. Saw an eighteen-hole golf course built on three levels with access by cable car.

13 October 1988 - SOUTH ISLAND

Jill and Mike were to stay on the North Island and I left them at Wellington and travelled across to Picton on the South Island. Arrived 1.45pm and caught the Delta Bus for Greymouth arriving at 7.45pm. Saw fantastic scenery, big rivers, mountains, falls and lakes. They have had the wettest year for very many years. Greymouth was flooded under five feet of water twice during the last two months. Rivers still very high. I missed Pancake Rocks where there was gold panning and a reproduction shantytown. Passed through Ross Goldfields, the origin of the largest gold nugget ever found in New Zealand, which was gifted to the Royal Family. The coach driver delivered papers and mail and he was carrying only a few passengers beside ourselves. I was in really hard country and it was difficult to find accommodation at Greymouth, walked a long way, eventually a taxi took me to a lovely family, Alan and Mary Owen a retired English couple put me up for the night and they took me the following morning to catch the early coach for the long journey to Franz Josef. Arrived approximately 11.00pm, very tired and found bed and breakfast for one night.

14 October 1988 (2nd day coach pass)
Still tired, a very scenic trip but some fog and rain. Coastal mountains, rain forest mixed in with snow and glaciers, rainfall is incredibly high at Franz Josef. Took helicopter trip to glacier, very good but foggy. Locals say best day for nearly two weeks. Franz Josef is a small place almost a ghost village, but the people were very friendly.

15 October 1988 (3rd day coach pass)
Leaving 8 am for Queenstown, heading toward Fox Glacier, couldn't see it but saw bends galore, waterfalls, rain forests, snow on the peaks, fog, rain and wind. Stopped at Bruce Bay on the coast, once a small, thriving gold mining village, now approximately two houses, water discoloured by glacier movement. Road built on swampland, hence very wary on travelling, saw three large lakes with good fishing, Lake Moeraki area and stopped at Knights Point to see some seals (no luck). The coastal road was opened in 1965 (it was a cattle pass before). When the road was built they found an English ship, which had foundered in Tasmania and had been swept by the strong current to this creek. Crossed the Haast River, a quarter of a mile wide and onto the Haast Pass 1,847 above sea level, gravel road for 25 miles. Passed over more rivers, a day with continual rain, wind and fog, unable to see the beauty except the waterfall and mountains near me.

16 October 1988

Was going to Milford Sound but the road has been closed by a landslide. Instead took a helicopter trip to view the scenery and then went on a large jetboat for about half an hour on Lake Wakatipu and River Kawarau. Took helicopter back to base.

Booked a white water rafting trip for 1.30pm, left base for Skippers Road gorge and canyon, the narrow road carved out of the side of the mountains is one of the world's most dangerous roads. Has dangerous bends and sheer drops, very scenic but dangerous. Huts on mountainside (ex-miners) are now shelter for hikers. Arrived on site with full kit, changed the by roadside into life jackets. Several rubber rafts, approximately eight people in each, took to the river, one guide in each raft who gave us a safety lecture before setting off. Guide of rafting scale = Grade 1: Easy, Grade 2: Medium, Grade 3: Difficult, Grade 4: Very Difficult, Grade 5: Extremely Difficult, 6: Unrunnable. We were on Grade 5 on the Shotover River gorge. I need say no more, two of our men were washed overboard and there were others who were swept out of their boats - other boats pulled them in. The river was swollen because of recent rains; one drop was approximately 12 feet. Another sheer drop put our boat nearly upright. We were at times full of water and had to bale out. The river dropped 200 feet in approximately one mile. Deep canyon, waterfalls. A gold mining barge boat was upside down in the river, had been there for some months. It will be raised when the river level drops. Near to the end of our one and half hour rafting a very large crowd watched us descend, and also photos were taken by the raft tour operators. We descended a very large fall into a mass of water, eventually completely full of water and we were out of control and crashed into another boat stuck on rocks in midstream, water was rushing everywhere, we just had to sit tight, hold on to the safety ropes and after moving across to the other boat eventually after 15 minutes approximately we bounced our way out. I shall never know how we steered to the shore. There was much congratulating after safely arriving and then it was back by truck to the hotel for a Jacuzzi, a change of clothes and some hot food and drink. Our party then went back to the tour office to see the photos; our guides did say that those rapids and the size of the river was rated by far the largest and most difficult in New Zealand. I'm glad I did it but never again.

All lakes in the Otago area are ex-glaciers, Lake Wakatipu, fifty miles long is New Zealand's longest lake and the lake is also very deep. The Moa bird (member of the Ostritch family) is according to local legend alleged to inhabit these remote parts but it was hunted to extinction in the nineteenth century. Gold mining in this region has now finished but the miners left dangerous shafts and now the region is known for its fruit orchards. Roaring Meg and Gender Anne were two infamous entertainment girls in the old mining days. Two rivers have been named after them. Individuals can still mine gold and some do, some are doing quite well in the Otago area. A Californian named Fox found gold in Arrowsmith. Gold is being mined there in large amounts.

17 October 1988

Left Queenstown for Dunedin and if weather permitted to go to Stewart Island, most southerly tip in the world. On the way to Dunedin the scenery was not so wild but saw sheep by the thousand. Saw lake Wakatipu again and the snow-capped mountains (the Remarkables), then on through sheep farming country, through Lumsden, Gore, Balclutha, Milton and finally to Dunedin. I had a last minute change of plan and decided not to stop at Dunedin but to go on to Christchurch by the coast road via Oamaru, Timaru, Ashburton and then to Christchurch arriving at 11 pm at the Ambassadors Hotel.

18 October 1988

Had an early morning call and my intention was to take the train over Arthurs Pass to Greymouth. Not possible on my coach pass (Intercity). Instead I walked to Christchurch City Square and climbed the cathedral steps to the top of the tower. I later took a bus tour of the city. I learnt some interesting facts of this beautiful garden city of 300,000 people. The Cathedral tower has 13 bells weighing 7 tons. There is a statue of Captain Scott and one of Queen Victoria. There are four trees in Cathedral Square of some historical significance. The weeping willows on the Avon river were brought from St Helena in the mid 19th century by the French. Hadley Park is the largest park at seven hundred acres. The Dean Bros from Kilmarnock, Scotland were the first settlers and it is the city museum, which is the oldest house where they once lived. I arranged a bus rather than a train so I left at 2 pm for Arthurs Pass en route to Greymouth. It was a very scenic drive indeed, with snow-capped mountains, winding roads and deep gorges and waterfalls. Also saw Highland cattle. After Arthurs Pass and down near the west coast passed through Kumara which has gold under the town. The Miners Royal Theatre is still there and so are the stage coach stops. Whitebait is caught in the Taramakau river. Passed Kumara racecourse which has one meeting per year and gets very crowded. Gold nuggets are given as prize money. Sunshine when we left, no more heavy rain. Went on to Reefton, staying the night arriving there late evening.

19 October 1988 (last day of coach pass)

Left the small town of Reefton at midday heading back for Christchurch. Interesting trip through more forests, rivers, mountains, and the Lewis Pass, did not go to the health resort at Hanmer Springs. Coach driver not very informative. Arrived Christchurch 5 pm, made contact by phone call to a Mr & Mrs Grigg, from nearby Ashburton. Picking me up from Ashburton bus station tomorrow morning at approximately 10.30am. Invited me to stay for a few days. Not related or not previously known to me except that prior research that I had made showed that their ancestors had emigrated from Cornwall and a John Grigg ancestor of theirs was a man of some importance locally

20 October 1988

Met Roger and his wife Margaret (now there's a coincidence) who showed me John Grigg's statue in the town. Took me to Long Beach where he arrived from Cornwall in the early 1800's. The Queen and the Duke of Edinburgh stayed at Long Beach. Stayed the night at Roger's farm and the following day he took me out with his land agent friend Ralph to see a farm which Roger is intending to buy having sold his previous farm. The asking price was £230,000 for 400 acres of rather stony land but it did have a good modern house and the land was good for farming sheep, deer or cattle. Farming is very depressed, farms are very cheap to buy compared to UK prices, New Zealand's farmers have to face the reality of world prices in their markets, there are no subsidies for them as we have in Europe and they also pay high interest rates to the bank.

21 October 1988
Went to the farm being sold again for a further inspection prior to Roger making an offer.
22 October 1988
Roger took me to Ashburton and met Ralph at his office, we then went to a farm to see it being sold by auction, 260 acres of very good land, grow malting, barley, biscuit wheat, peas, and with a good house. Irrigated with it's own water and was sold for £100,000, very cheap compared to back home. Took me to another farm of a friend which had heavier soil but grows very good crops, two tons plus per acre for wheat and also grows clover and ryegrass. In the evening we all went to a party where some prizes were being presented.
23 October 1988
Back on the road again. No time to let the grass to grow under my feet. Said goodbye to the Grigg's and their wonderful hospitality. Left Ashburton at 5.30am for the one hour trip to Christchurch and took off at 8.00am for the two hour flight to Melbourne. Spent the next few nights with John and Jean Cocks at Bacchus Marsh in the fruit growing region near Melbourne. The Cocks were friends of Jane and Leo and it had been arranged that I should visit them.
24 October 1988
They took me to Ballarat and we drove through some good farming country. I had a tour of the mining town, the museum, saw the old costumes, coach horses, steam engines and some working pumps. I also had a go at panning for some minute amounts of gold. Bought my Acubra hat and some T-shirts for presents back home.
25 October 1988
Had a day sightseeing in Melbourne
26 October 1988
Went to a cattle market fifty miles away and also saw where Margaret and John Cocks brother-in-law was going to build a house. Returned to Melbourne with the brother in law. And I went on a tour to see more of Melbourne. John and Margaret took me to the airport late in the evening and I left for Bangkok on a nine hour flight just after midnight.

THAILAND - BANGKOK

27 October 1988
Stayed at Hotel Manohra. Very tired, slept most of the day, and I missed the coach trip to the Palace. Eventually got up and went to the bank for Bahts. Arranged for a taxi the following day

28 October 1988
Taxi picked me up, took me to the river to catch a sight seeing trip by boat. It was a three hours round trip and it was very interesting to see how the people lived and worked in such terrible conditions. Saw mills, timber drifting to mills, houses being awash, trading in food, bananas, flowers, boys swimming, jumping on and off boats. Visited the market place and bought a crocodile handbag and scarf, then to a snake farm and a snake show, snakes were held in the mouth and in each hand. Returned to Bangkok via The Orient Hotel (best in world) and I took photos of temples by the river. The taxi took me to see the Golden Temple where there is a solid gold Buddha, 700 years old, weighing 5,550 kg. There are 30,000 temples in Thailand, 3,000 approximately in Bangkok. I saw the Kings Royal Palace which was really fantastic and I took several photos. The king stays here for one hundred days before throning. The body of a dead king will lie in state in the west side of the temple before being cremated in the temple. The old parliament is now being used as a museum. The New Parliament building is nearby. Went to a silk factory, bought a headscarf and also to a precious stone factory and shop.

Bridge over the river Kwai

29 October 1988

Left 7.00am for the 120 kilometre trip to the River Kwai on Death Railway. On the way through Bangkok the train passed through Chinatown with about 30,000 Chinese inhabitants. There is a huge flower market there every morning.

At The Bridge over the Kwai saw the Museum of Tortures to Allied prisoners by the Japs. The railway is 415 kilometre in length, going through both Burma and Thailand. Construction began on 16 September 1942 at Moog Pladook by approximately 30,000 prisoners of war and 100,000 impressed labourers from Imara, Malaysia and other countries; of these more than 16,000 prisoners died through disease etc. It was supposed to take five years to build, the Japanese army forced the prisoners and it was finished in sixteen months, on 25 December 1943. I took a rail trip to the Burmese frontier. Before that we had a boat trip up the River Kwai to a cemetery of prisoners. Left railway to have lunch and visit the waterfall. Returned to Bangkok after this in time for going out again to a show that evening.

Went out on a tictuc (a three wheel tricycle taxi) which gave me quite a scary ride through the congested streets.

30 October 1988

Left the Hotel Manohra in late morning for the Queens Hotel in Pattaya, arrived 5.00pm. Met a Canadian salesman from the steel industry and a Dutch detective loaned to the Philippines. Went to see a Thai boxing contest where the boxing is done with the feet. Went to see an evening show at Tiffany's which was very good.

31 October 1988
This was my last day in Thailand and I made good use of it to do as much sightseeing as possible. I took a trip to the ornamental gardens, watched traditional Thai dancing, saw cock fighting, sword fighting and for a final event to bring my holiday to a close I rode an elephant and then as a final act in the elephant display I allowed myself to be chosen from the audience to be walked over by an elephant .

The next day it was a flight back to London. In September I had basically seen all of Australia from North to South, East to West and the heart of Australia at Alice Springs. I had bought for nine hundred Australian dollars a ten thousand kilometre go anywhere ticket. These were my flights noted below and the total distance was just under the ten thousand kilometre limit. Brisbane to Cairns. Cairns to Darwin. Darwin to Alice Springs. Alice Springs to Perth. Perth to Adelaide and finally Adelaide to Sydney. I then travelled onto New Zealand and spent a further three weeks there seeing most of the country, back to Melbourne for a few days and then finally five days in Thailand. I think I must have been making up for lost time. Other than my trip to Canada and to China a few years earlier I had never really travelled before. I enjoyed travel and I had the urge to do a lot more. But it was now time to go back home.

A Tribute
William (Bill) Herbert Grigg

26 March 1920 - 8 May 1998

Today I stand here as a representative of a family united in grief.

We have all come to pay our respects and give thanks for the life of a man I am so proud to be able to call my father. Each and everyone of us that are here and those that are not able to be here today will remember him in their own special way.

We pay tribute to you Bill, my father, a truly gentle man giving a touchstone of definition to the words, "He was a real gentleman".

Today is our chance to say thank you for the way you enriched our lives, a man of compassion, a symbol of selfless humanity, a classless man.

To me, besides being a wonderful father, you were also a source of strength and inspiration. You were my true friend.

He gave selflessly to others, he would always down tools to attend those in need of help, in time of sickness or personal difficulties.

He too had his own share of difficulties but he lived through them, overcame them.

The true measure of his worth, the source of my deepest love and admiration, is that no matter the obstacles and adversities, he never lost his personal dignity, his compassion and humanity shone through. Indeed you gave so much of your heart that come the end you had so little left for yourself.

We pay tribute to his loving wife, Margaret, and mother of four of his five children. To her undying love and eternal devotion throughout their long thick and thin marriage and beyond.

We as a family wish to pay tribute to his partner Carole. For the love, the wonderful, wonderful care, the close companionship. She so selflessly gave him that most precious of gifts: extra time – to spend here with us.

He was a man of indomitable spirit: only ten years ago, when nearly seventy, he climbed Ayers Rock in the Australian outback, walked the Great Wall of China and rode the white water rapids of New Zealand.

He had his moments of glory and achievement:

In horse racing: you had stood as the proud owner in the winner's enclosure at the Cheltenham Festival.

In business: the success you enjoyed in the 1980s in property development in Plymouth where you spent most of the last fifteen years.

In farming: in youthful years, with your late brother, at St. Mabyn, growing vegetables for the London market, and a lifetime farming at your beloved Fentrigan, which in recent years you passed on to your younger son.

And finally and most significantly in the last months and years the writing of a book. No small achievement for someone of poor health.

Perhaps in the end, in your life's final chapter, you did find your true vocation.

It is all there, condensed into the written word. A most interesting life of a very remarkable man who lived through a period of history of amazing changes.

You were an eternal optimist, to you the bottle was always half full, and not half empty.

You tried your best to live by high ideals.

Kipling's IF was written with such a man as you in mind.

Reluctantly, sadly, we surrender you back. We will remember you, Always.

IF

If you can keep your head when all about you
Are losing theirs and blaming it on you,
If you can trust yourself when all men doubt you
But make allowance for their doubting too,
If you can wait and not be tired by waiting,
Or being lied about, don't deal in lies,
Or being hated, don't give way to hating,
And yet don't look too good, nor talk too wise:
If you can dream--and not make dreams your master,
If you can think--and not make thoughts your aim;
If you can meet with Triumph and Disaster
And treat those two impostors just the same;
If you can bear to hear the truth you've spoken
Twisted by knaves to make a trap for fools,
Or watch the things you gave your life to, broken,
And stoop and build 'em up with worn-out tools:
If you can make one heap of all your winnings
And risk it all on one turn of pitch-and-toss,
And lose, and start again at your beginnings
And never breath a word about your loss;
If you can force your heart and nerve and sinew
To serve your turn long after they are gone,
And so hold on when there is nothing in you
Except the Will which says to them: "Hold on!"
If you can talk with crowds and keep your virtue,
Or walk with kings--nor lose the common touch,
If neither foes nor loving friends can hurt you;
If all men count with you, but none too much,
If you can fill the unforgiving minute
With sixty seconds' worth of distance run,
Yours is the Earth and everything that's in it,
And--which is more--you'll be a Man, my son!
--Rudyard Kipling